Praise for **ANOTHER APPALACHIA**

"*Another Appalachia* is a breath of fresh air, a work that the public is in dire need of reading. Wide and expansive as the land the author calls home, this essay collection subverts the mainstream's hyperfocus on white male-dominated narratives from rural America and commands your attention from the first page to the last word."

— Morgan Jerkins, author of *This Will Be My Undoing: Living at the Intersection of Black, Female, and Feminist in (White) America* and *Caul Baby*

"Neema Avashia, in this book, has named the unnamed, spoken the unspoken so that it does not become—to paraphrase Adrienne Rich—the unspeakable, and she has done so in language that is both lyrical and direct, both entertaining and edifying, both challenging and generous. I love this book and believe it introduces an important voice in America's ongoing racial reckoning."

— Rahul Mehta, author of *No Other World*

"An essential text to add to the new canon of Appalachian writing—a compassionate and rigorous memoir of the author's experience growing up as a queer Hindu child and teenager in a small community of West Virginian Indians. *Another Appalachia* is a bright and deeply empathetic portrait of a complicated place, a place that Neema Avashia allows to be multifaceted in the way it deserves."

— Anna Claire Weber, White Whale Bookstore

T0054652

ANOTHER APPALACHIA

COMING UP QUEER AND INDIAN IN A MOUNTAIN PLACE

NEEMA AVASHIA

WEST VIRGINIA UNIVERSITY PRESS

MORGANTOWN

ISBN 978-1-952271-42-7 (paperback) / 978-1-952271-43-4 (ebook)

Library of Congress Control Number: 2021046869

Book and cover design by Than Saffel / WVU Press
Cover image courtesy of the author

Lines from "Heritage" © James Still, *From the Mountain, From the Valley: New and Collected Poems* (Lexington: University Press of Kentucky, 2014)

Lines from "Kentucke" © Frank X Walker, *Affrilachia: Poems by Frank X Walker* (Lexington: Old Cove Press, 2000)

Essays in this collection previously appeared in the following publications: "Directions to a Vanishing Place," *Women Speak*, vol. 4, 10th anniversary collection, Women of Appalachia Project, 2019; "Chemical Bonds," *Kenyon Review Online*, May/June 2020; "Nine Forms of the Goddess," *Hong Kong Review*, vol. 1, no. 1, winter 2018; "Be Like Wilt," *Bitter Southerner*, November 2019; "The Blue-Red Divide," *Kestrel*, winter 2019; "Finding the Holy in an Unholy Coconut," *Superstition Review*, issue 23, spring 2019; "Wine Warmth," *Still: The Journal*, winter 2018; "A Hindu Hillbilly Elegy," *Longridge Review*, October 2019; "Neighbors," *Still: The Journal*, October 2019; "Shame-Shame," *Cosmonauts Avenue*, July 2020; "Present-Life Hair" as "How a Haircut Helped Me Untangle My Identity as a Queer Indian Woman," *Catapult*, June 2020

⊙⊙⊙⊙⊙⊙

CONTENTS

⚘ ⚘ ⚘

⊙⊙⊙⊙⊙⊙

Directions to a Vanishing Place

ᴥ ⟟ ᴥ

○○◎◎○○

Drive west on I-64, away from the airport named Yeager, carved into a mountaintop, away from the capitol dome coated in gold, away from the cruelly nicknamed "Needle City" with its shuttered buildings and staggering addiction numbers. Just 15.9 miles down the road, in between the exits for Institute and Nitro, right after the Pink Pony strip club, you hit exit 47. The exit for Cross Lanes, West Virginia.

The exit for the place you call home.

Cross Lanes: once the bedroom community for management at the chemical plants that sprung up along the Kanawha River during World War II. Now the plants have closed, and the community shrinks each year.

Hang a right off the exit ramp.

Pass:

A gas station.

Another gas station.

A bank.

A third gas station.

A hair salon.

Hit the drive-thru at Tudor's Biscuit World, home of the Eighth Wonder of the culinary world: a hash brown smothered with bottled cheese, sandwiched between two halves of biscuit. In high school, you would skip class in search of this delicacy, the only vegetarian item on the menu.

At the one stoplight in town, continue onto Big Tyler Road.

Pass the National Institute of Technology building. Your dad used to say you'd end up there if you didn't get your grades up. The bank-turned-Black megachurch Temple of Faith Ministries, where T. D. Jakes birthed his career as a televangelist. Lower Sun Valley Drive, where country music singer Kathy Mattea grew up. Upper Sun Valley Drive, where your best friend's family, with its six hardy children, used to shovel out the entire street during snowstorms rather than pay for a plow.

Pass:

A pawn shop whose parking lot is always filled with cars.

The bar whose name has changed at least thirteen times since it opened.

Your middle school alma mater: Andrew Jackson.

Linger for just a minute here at the fields and courts of your youth. Every weekend from April to October, kids in stiff polyester uniforms perched on the pitcher's mound and bases. The sound of rubber basketball hitting pavement, then backboard, then swishing through the net was a steady presence on hot summer days.

Now, the infield is covered with weeds, the bases have been excavated, the grandstand is boarded up, even though it's peak season for Little League baseball. Beside the field, four poles reach skyward, giving the semblance and structure of a basketball court, but no backboards or nets exist. Tall grass emerges from the cracks in the concrete.

Continue on your journey past Mousie's Car Wash, then make the familiar right turn into West Gate, whose big iron gates perpetually stand open. For Sale signs litter the grass, each with a different real estate agent's name and phone number.

The developer named every street in the neighborhood after his daughters—Karen, Dawn, Pamela, Ann. All of the houses share the same blueprint: 3 bedrooms, 2.5 bathrooms, finished basements. Even twenty years after moving out, you could stand blindfolded at the front door of any house in the neighborhood and walk through it without stumbling.

Head straight down Dawn Street, take a left on Karen Circle, then finally a right onto Pamela Circle. Drive past the house that was yours throughout childhood, acquired by parents who were known as Rita and "Doc" to everyone in the neighborhood. A tiny, maroon-and-white hand-painted sign written in your mom's distinctive Gujarati-turned-English script announces the house number—5303. The garden has been replaced by grass, the basketball hoop torn down, your mom's unruly mint patch mowed over. No trace remains of the giant American flag your father taped on the door after 9/11. Of your parents' immense efforts to Americanize, only the rose bushes endure.

Descend the gradual slope of Pamela Circle where you learned to ride your bike. Your uncle's Bata sandals flapped as he ran alongside you. He held the seat to help you stay upright, didn't let go 'til you told him you were ready.

Skim over the patch of warm concrete where you lay in the summertime and stared at the multitude of stars shimmering on a navy-blue blanket of sky.

Pass the Lunardinis' house, where you taught baby Nick to say "ball" by tossing a basketball up and down in front of his bedroom window every morning on your way down the street to shoot hoops. Pass Mr. Woody's garage, where he taxidermied animals whose beady glass eyes sometimes still haunt you in your sleep.

Pass the porches where you used to sit with Mr. Starcher and Mr. Casto in the evenings, your eleven-year-old self nodding along sagely as they discussed the day's news.

Occasionally, when talk of the plant came up, you'd interject with commentary pilfered from your dad's frustrated night-time phone calls.

Pass the double hill between the Carneys' and Mundays' houses, where you whiled away hours of childhood. Summers, you played King of the Mountain, wrestling with your friends for positioning at the top of the hill. Winters, you crashed your sled into the icy creek with glee, then hauled it back up the hill and rushed back down again.

Pass the streetlight that marked home base during games of Spotlight every night of every summer between six and sixteen. Its daily illumination coincided with your mom yelling down the street that dinner was ready and you needed to come home.

Pass the two basketball hoops, diagonally placed, where you would play for hours. Barefoot in the summertime, in snow boots in the winter. Lee, Wes, and Andy were your steadfast playmates in these games. But early mornings with Mr. Withrow are what you remember most. The red-headed surrogate American dad who shot hoops with you, gave you driving lessons, grew figs and rhubarb for you. He died asleep in his armchair a few years ago, but you can still hear the triumphant cry he made every time he scored a bucket: "The banks are open!"

Stop, for just a moment, at Mrs. Carney's house. One of the only neighbors from childhood still living on the street, her golden hair is whiter, her body smaller, every time you visit. You sip her famous sun tea, and she updates you on the lives of the people who once populated this street: those who have moved, those who have married, those who have died. Stare hard at the pink carpet, the antique walnut secretary desk, the grandfather clock, the paintings on the walls. The house feels empty without the sound of Mr. Carney's warm voice inviting you in for meandering chats that would sometimes start before the sun went down and not end until after the moon came up.

Near the end of Pamela Circle, the last house on the street once belonged to a smiling family torn apart by divorce in the late nineties. Now, the single-story house, red brick with white trim, has come off its foundation and edges toward a sinkhole. The windows are boarded up and an eviction notice on the door declares the house uninhabitable. The ramshackle conditions of abandoned mining communities in the southern part of the state creep onto the very street where you once lived.

Drive out of West Gate, past the roses, the basketball hoops, the streetlights, the plywood over windows, the grass coming through cracks in concrete, the headless basketball hoops, the endless rows of For Sale signs. Head back down Big Tyler Road onto the ramp for I-64, away from the legions of loved ones who are slowly leaving too.

Chemical Bonds

In India, during his rural medicine rotation in the late 1960s, my father lived in a village terrorized by rabid dogs. They travelled in packs, chasing children, biting bicyclists, infecting the villagers with rabies. These villagers became paranoid, delirious, and hydrophobic, deteriorated into a comatose state, and then died, in the span of just a few weeks.

There was no money for vaccines, so my father purchased arsenic with his own meager savings. Mixed it with milk. Poured the poison into stainless steel bowls and placed the bowls around the village, knowing the rabid dogs would hungrily lap up the milk. For days afterwards, the bodies of dead dogs littered the streets, but the patients in the waiting room at my father's clinic no longer foamed at the mouth.

In my father's moral calculus, the lives of humans are always worth more than the lives of animals. And what counts as poison for some is inoculation for the many.

This is the worldview of a physician employed by a chemical plant for over thirty years: DDT kills mosquitoes, preventing the spread of debilitating diseases like malaria, dengue, and chikungunya. Asbestos stops the spread of fire in school buildings, hospitals, and homes. Methyl isocyanate kills insects, allowing crops to flourish. Chemicals prevent illness. Chemicals spur our nourishment. Chemicals save lives.

Any accidents that happen are simply that—accidents. And no accident outweighs the benefits that chemicals confer. For my immigrant father, raised in poverty in the developing world, chemicals were a godsend, both in their concrete use and in the employment they provided him.

This is the bedtime story that my father told me every night when I was a child. This is the story I believed well into adulthood, until, all at once, I didn't.

* * *

After medical school, my father immigrated to the United States in 1969, first settling in Queens for his residency in occupational medicine, and then, four years later, taking a job at the Union Carbide plant in Institute, West Virginia. I cannot count the number of times in my life I have been asked the question "Why West Virginia?" by disbelieving Americans who can't envision West Virginia as a state with any amount of diversity. But at the time, Indian immigrants did not have extensive options. They most often found work in the places where privileged Americans would not venture, in the midst of either urban or rural poverty.

Put simply, my father needed a job. West Virginia was closer than Seadrift, Texas, his other option. And on their first visit, my parents found the lush greenery and mountains of the Mountain State, so different from dry and dusty Gujarat, deeply alluring.

They moved into a three-bedroom, two-and-a-half-bathroom house on a street called Pamela Circle, situated in a planned development called West Gate. West Gate was one of many such developments in the bedroom community of Cross Lanes, built specifically to house the managerial workers of the chemical industry. Add two kids, a fenced-in yard with a giant garden, a sky-blue Dodge Dart, and a growing bank account, and all the needed ingredients for the American Dream suddenly fell into place for my family. Thanks, in no small part, to Union Carbide.

"Doc," as most West Virginians quickly dubbed my dad, was deeply respected in the community: quick tempered, for sure, but also educated, generous, and neighborly. The kind of man who gave flu shots to the family and the neighbors, then drove around town administering them to the grocer, the tire shop guys, and the auto mechanic, and who conducted physical exams for all the kids on the street so that families wouldn't have to pay to see their primary care physician. The kind of man who would bring back prescription medicine from India, because it was available cheaply and without prescription, and give it to the people in our community who needed it most. He sought, at every turn, to make himself useful, both because that was how he was raised and because usefulness is the ultimate survival strategy for immigrants in America.

Our neighbors responded in turn, always at the ready when the garden needed to be rototilled, the car needed an oil change, or my sister and I needed to learn a skill that my immigrant parents were not prepared to teach—like driving or shooting hoops or using power tools.

My father's ethics were not typical, and certainly might have been frowned on by the medical establishment, but at the time, I understood them as the ethics of place: Being a good neighbor, and by extension a good person, meant giving 100 percent of what you had to the community where you lived. The "rules" mattered less than the impact of your actions.

This ethic of place followed me into my professional life as a teacher. I have taught at my school for nearly two decades and am as firmly rooted there as I was on Pamela Circle. Many of my current students are the third or fourth sibling in families that I've been teaching since 2003. Where my dad attended every wedding, anniversary celebration, and funeral of people who worked at the chemical plant, I attend the quinceañeras, graduation cookouts, and, tragically, funerals of former students on a regular basis. I am the writer of recommendation letters, the reference on job applications, the 0 percent interest moneylender, and the advisor on big decisions for hundreds of young people across the city of Boston. This does not feel optional for me. It feels like the way I am supposed to do my job, because that is how my father did his.

* * *

In the early morning hours of December 3, 1984, my father received a panicked phone call from a high-powered executive at the corporate headquarters of the Union Carbide Corporation, the chemical plant where he was employed as the company doctor. Thirty tons of toxic methyl isocyanate had leaked from the Carbide compound in Bhopal, India, killing between four thousand and fifteen thousand people, and severely burning and blinding thousands more, most of whom used the solid brick wall of the plant compound as a firm backing for their otherwise flimsy tin and plastic shanties. Carbide needed to send a crisis team to India. They wanted my Indian father to be part of their otherwise White team.

I think of my father, aged thirty-nine, close to the same age I am now. With two young children, a mortgage, parents and siblings to financially support in India, and a keen sense of being the brown-skinned foreigner with the funny accent trying desperately to assimilate into working-class Appalachian culture. What would he have lost if he said no? What would he gain by saying yes?

My father accepted his role as the token, went to Bhopal, acted as the face of Union Carbide in front of the global media and the Indian government. In the midst of thousands of his burned, blinded countrymen, in the midst of bodies strewn in the streets as dogs had once been in that village long ago, he sided with the company that signed his paycheck over the country of his birth. He embraced chemicals as the path to security and success, for himself and for his family. He has held chemicals in that embrace ever since, never failing to come to their defense.

* * *

For the first twelve years of my teaching career, my approach to the work only merited accolades. I taught a history methods course for student teachers to prepare them to work in the Boston Public Schools. I wrote the civics curriculum for the entire school district and ran professional development sessions training other teachers in how to use it. My classroom, with its clothesline of brightly colored T-shirts emblazoned with radical protest slogans, became a site for new teachers to observe as they honed their craft. In 2013, the school district recognized me as one of Boston's Educators of the Year.

The following year, the district selected me, along with only two other teachers, to serve as members of the incoming superintendent's transition team, tasked with crafting a new vision for the work of the Boston Public Schools. I felt my voice, and my influence, growing. Friends in other schools often described feeling like they were "widgets": unseen and unknown by a district that viewed them as numbers rather than humans. I understood their experience but couldn't relate. I wasn't a widget, or so I thought.

Then, in 2016, the school district released budget proposals for individual schools, and we learned that my school faced over one million dollars in budget cuts. We stood to lose half of our arts department, much-needed special education teachers, and some of our strongest teachers of academic content. Our staff rallied, went to budget hearings, and gave passionate testimony explaining the impact of such deep cuts on our school. Still, the budget proposal remained unchanged.

Frightened by the depth of the cuts, and certain that they foretold the approaching death of our school community, I reached out to a local newspaper and asked them to write a story. The *Bay State Banner* printed a piece about the impact of budget cuts, with a giant picture of my face running on the front page.

The day after the piece dropped, my awkward rookie principal called me into his office after school. He'd been contacted by his bosses, who had asked him to deliver a message:

"All communication with media needs to be cleared through BPS communications."

What happened next is unclear. Did he fumble his words? Did I mishear him? I could swear that he said, "Otherwise, you risk losing your job."

He claims he said, "Otherwise, *I* could risk losing *my* job."

I stared at him, flabbergasted. "I can't lose my job for speaking to the press," I said, the civics teacher in me growing more outraged by the moment. "Freedom of speech is protected for public school employees. There was a whole Supreme Court case about it in 1968."

He shrugged helplessly. "I'm just passing on the message I was given."

I left his office and called our union organizer. "I just got told to stop speaking to media without permission from BPS or I will lose my job," I told her.

The next morning, the union president wrote a blurb in our e-newsletter describing the incident, stridently clarifying the free speech rights of public school teachers. By midday, the *Boston Globe* had posted a story with the headline

"Union Accuses Boston School Department of Trying to Silence Teachers."

That afternoon, the superintendent of the Boston Public Schools called me on my commute home, asking, "Couldn't you have resolved this internally? Why did you feel the need to take it public?"

The impact mattered more than the rules. This is what I had grown up believing. Now I was being told that following the rules of silence and subordination mattered more than protecting the health of my community.

"I did try to resolve it internally," I told him. "We went to you. We went to the School Committee. We begged you to listen, and you didn't change anything. So then we took it public."

After this, I was no longer the favored teacher of the establishment. I transformed into someone new, someone different: someone feared for my ability to create shame within district leadership. And fear made people listen in a different way. When I emailed the superintendent with a concern, he responded immediately. I got pulled into meetings with higher-ups on a regular basis regarding issues ranging from youth violence to school police cooperation with Immigration and Customs Enforcement. The district's strategy for reining me in was to pull me closer rather than push me away.

The school district did not ultimately restore our funds, but the experience taught me something my father had been unable to: that sometimes, acting ethically on behalf of my community required fighting against, rather than alongside, my employer.

* * *

My dad and I do not talk about our family's tangled history with chemicals. In truth, we don't talk much at all about topics that fall outside the bounds of the following three themes: financial investments, dead and dying West Virginian loved ones, and the weather in Texas, where he now lives. This dynamic is not new. When I was a kid, my dad assigned me *Wall Street Journal* articles to read and then required me to share summaries and reactions with him before dinner. His bedtime stories always included a hygiene moral, usually about the importance of brushing one's teeth. His great-grandfather left the family to study law and never returned. His father, my grandfather, did not express emotion even when we visited him after five years of absence. Without models of what deep father-child bonds could look like, my dad did the best he could. Still, our conversations run more educational and transactional than they do emotional.

Every time I have written about him, I've been asked in workshop to include scenes between us. But I don't see my father in scene. I see him in monologue: My dad speaking, me listening, and then him abruptly hanging up the phone or leaving the room when he tires of talking. Some of this is generational, some of it is gendered, some of it is cultural, but the notion of my father talking *with* me about his history or his beliefs is simply something I haven't experienced. He has talked *at* me, and I can summarize those ideas deftly, but scene eludes me. Scene implies an exchange of ideas, and there is no exchange between my father and me: He has his ideas, I have mine. Never the twain shall meet.

Searching for ways to bring my father's voice into this piece, I turned to the archives of the *Charleston Gazette*, the main newspaper for our community in West Virginia. I found a piece written by my father in 2015. Twelve years after leaving the valley, he, too, still mulls on this history. The piece, entitled "Remembering a Better West Virginia," was published on the seventieth anniversary of the end of World War II and is an amalgam of all the snippets my father has repeated to me time and time again.

During the war chemical companies were asked by our elected government to make goods needed for the war effort. At the end of the war they could have laid off everybody. But instead, they re-purposed these chemical facilities to make ingredients that make latex paint, crayons, detergents, soaps, and shampoos. They made rubber additives that made tires and rubber belts last longer and made driving safer. They made swimming pools cleaner and chemicals that farmers and the home gardeners could safely use to produce the crops that fed the world . . .

A couple of dozen cases of Mesothelioma from asbestos occurred, but balance that against hundreds of people who did not get burns from hot processes and leaks that did not occur from asbestos gaskets. In those days, safer substitutes were not yet invented . . .

Books have been written on workplace tragedies. But I could easily write a book on how a Clay County kid came to Charleston, got a job to collect samples from production units on bicycle and quickly delivered them to a lab for analysis. This kid soon realized the path to upward mobility was education. He took classes at Morris Harvey College to get his degree to become a chemist, finally becoming the manager for environmental affairs. He retired and became an industry consultant for several more years. And this story was repeated by many.

Today, Kanawha Valley's chemical industry is a minuscule shadow of the chemical center of the world it billed itself to be back then. The chemical workers were able to afford houses and usually two cars, send their children to colleges in West Virginia, who in turn came back as doctors, engineers and lawyers. Every year there were summer jobs galore. Industry paid property taxes and state government did not require across the board cuts, and charities in town from symphony to Salvation Army and local church's collection plates met their needs. Car dealers and real estate agents were happy to see the customer traffic every other year when the Carbide savings plan paid out. At Carbide camps, children of the managers played with the children of operators for $25 per week. Even Bernie Sanders can support that.

How did we get in this situation?

West Virginia politicians did next to nothing when a small number of lawyers relentlessly attacked industry, thinking that industry would not go away. Multiple class actions and other litigation only helped defense and plaintiff lawyers. . . . Big chemical giants are gone, replaced by the likes of Freedom Industries. Shelter-in-place for a few hours was nothing compared to what the newcomers have done. The chemical industry in the valley is on its last leg. There is not enough volume left to support cost-effective production. The future is bleak for the industry, and with little new industry coming in, I fear for the Kanawha Valley as well.

The chemical industry wasn't perfect, by far. But one has to look at the balance of good and bad. I know this piece will echo the sentiments of many Valley residents.

My father is something of an absolutist when it comes to chemicals, rejecting litigation as a means to greater safety and regulation, in much the same way that I can be an absolutist when it comes to education. No doubt he wishes I had a more nuanced view of charter schools and standardized testing, both of which I reject.

In turn, I, too, wish for him to possess more nuance: to acknowledge, for once, that simply boiling the water will not cleanse the Elk River of the ten thousand gallons of crude 4-methylcyclohexanemethanol (a chemical foam used to wash coal) that Freedom Industries poured into it in 2014.

That no amount of heat could strip the contaminated water of its vomit-inducing, liver- and kidney-damaging properties. I wish he would explain why he thought it was a good idea to spray my head with the pesticide Sevin when I came home from school with lice in second grade. I want to know whether we kept eating vegetables from our garden when the Carbide plant in Institute leaked methyl isocyanate into the West Virginia air in 1985, just six months after Bhopal. Even after government officials declared that people should not eat homegrown produce because of its exposure to contaminants, I don't remember our tomatoes dying on the vine.

* * *

In October of 2018, representatives of the Boston Public Schools convened a meeting with our staff and told us that our school would be closing after the 2019–2020 school year. That our students would be sent to an underperforming school a mile away—a high school already struggling to serve its existing students without the added complication of middle schoolers. That our school building would be renovated and given over to another school. That "there was no plan" for our staff. We would need to find other work as best we could.

In other words, we were being evicted. Without cause. Without a plan for mitigating the impacts of closure.

In my rage over the blatant lack of respect for the students and staff at my school, I turned to Twitter and exposed the fallacies in the district's plan. I stood up at School Committee meetings and gave history lessons about what has happened when underperforming schools have been asked to take on more students, adding complexity to their already full plates. I purchased twenty copies of Eve Ewing's book *Ghosts in the Schoolyard: Racism and School Closings on Chicago's South Side* and theatrically assigned required reading to the School

Committee members, demanding that they learn about the impact of school closures on the students of Chicago before voting to enact similar pain on the children of Boston. I wrapped myself in the First Amendment and spoke to every journalist who expressed even the slightest interest in telling the story of how wrongheaded, and how racist, this school closure process was.

If my father had been the epitome of the company man for Union Carbide, I was quickly becoming his opposite. The Norma Rae of the Boston Public Schools. The Ralph Nader of school closures. The very kind of person my father expressed exasperation with when I was growing up. My father did not suffer rabble-rousers gladly, and I was starting to be the loudest rabble-rouser in town.

"What do I have to lose?" I asked my partner Laura the night after the closure announcement. "They've already stated their intent to destroy my community and strip me of my job. What do I gain by staying silent?"

My initial fight-or-flight response after the announcement had been to consider quitting. Leaving the teaching profession altogether. Why should I continue to work for Boston Public Schools, an organization that didn't value our community or our work? Laura allowed me to spin through the "flight" options without commenting.

Now, she smiled. "There's the Neema I've been waiting for. The McCormack is your home. You don't give up your home without a fight."

I tweeted and spoke recklessly, but underneath my recklessness lay confidence and moral clarity. Confidence that I possessed a safety net: my own financial security, my professional relationships, and the generational wealth my father's loyalty to the chemical industry had made possible. Moral clarity about the fact that the district's plan was harmful to young people and required serious modification.

Chemicals paved the road from my immigrant father's mythologized arrival in the United States with eight dollars in his pocket to my citizen father's seven-figure investment account. My father's embrace of chemicals gave birth to my privilege. I am not confused about this fact.

I know I will continue to thrive if my school closes and I have to find another job. My undocumented students, my working-class students, my students who have experienced trauma, on the other hand, might not. The impact of school closures on academic performance, on dropout rates, on young people's emotional health is both well documented and damning. When we disconnect young people from school communities, we separate them from second homes and second families. We remove their safety net and then are surprised by their self-destructive and community-destroying behaviors. The conditions adults create for young people ultimately shape who those young people end up becoming. My father had not spoken up for his countrymen because doing so would have put his family's financial security at risk. This fact, and my own lack of financial peril, impelled me further to speak up for mine.

I picked up my father from the airport on the Tuesday before Thanksgiving. He got into the car while I was in the middle of a phone call with an area journalist, updating her on the changes in the plan for my school. The Boston Public Schools has walked back their plan in the face of our community's onslaught. We are no longer being evicted, but rather having our building renovated while we continue to work and learn there. We will seek applications from high schools looking to merge with us, instead of our building being handed over to a high school while our community gets dismantled. Once a marriage is successfully arranged between our community and a prospective high school, we will share the building as a unified 7–12 high school. Slowly, painstakingly, we are making progress. Progress that would have been impossible had we not chosen to fight.

After I ended the call, my dad commented, "Don't get too involved with all of this, Neema. You can't control what they will end up doing."

In a conversation with my mom earlier in the month, she echoed a similar sentiment. "Don't let yourself get too stressed about this. There is nothing you can do."

When my parents initially made these statements, I grew annoyed with them. Rather than supporting me, both sought, in their own ways, to quash my resistance. In the moment, I understood their comments as an effort to protect me from myself and, ultimately, from getting fired. Only later did I wonder, How often had they said these very words to each other as young Indian immigrants navigating all-White spaces in West Virginia? Toeing the company line had been their survival strategy; bucking it was mine. The distance between our experiences—theirs as first-generation immigrants navigating a world dominated by Whiteness, mine as a natural-born citizen chafing against systemic racism—felt as vast as the eight-thousand-mile flight from Mumbai to New York must have felt the first time my parents took that journey.

I once viewed my father's ethics as the ethics of community. Now I wondered if in fact they had been the ethics of assimilation, or the ethics of survival.

* * *

By 2001, the Union Carbide Corporation had been completely dismantled through a series of sell-offs and mergers that left it in shambles. Some pointed to NAFTA and outsourcing as the cause of Carbide's demise. Others attributed the company's downfall to increased environmental regulations and associated costs, making it difficult to turn a profit.

Of course, if you ever listened to his call-ins to talk radio under the pseudonym "Al," you would know that my father blames the disappearance of Carbide from the Chemical Valley on short-sighted lawyers and litigious West Virginians, eager to make any money they could off the slightest whiff of chemicals in the air: a legacy of Bhopal.

My father believed in corporate benevolence. He trusted that his bosses, and their bosses, would ultimately make decisions that benefited employees and the community, and not just the bottom line. And maybe in the 1970s, when he was first introduced to corporate America, that was true. Maybe. Or maybe the corruption was just harder to see, because he did not have access to the offices full of good ol' boys where the backroom deals were being made.

I want to tell my father that everything he believes about the power of chemicals is true. But also that DDT poisons the birds and the fish and the water, eventually finding its carcinogenic way into the very cellular structures of our bodies. Infinitesimal asbestos fibers, so easy to inhale, irritate the lung lining and make it difficult to breathe, and are the only known cause of mesothelioma. Methyl isocyanate burns our eyes, our nostrils, our lungs, our skin, gives us nausea and blurred vision, kills us if we are close enough to the site of exposure. Chemicals are both the balm and the poison.

I want to tell him things he already knows but refuses to say out loud. That companies, and governments, cannot be trusted to do what is right for civilians. That civilians will only achieve just ends when they speak up. That no matter how much we try, we will never be viewed as insiders in America. That we need to embrace our outsider status, and use it to fight.

My father outlasted the Carbide sell-offs until 2003, when he was given two options: leave the Chemical Valley, now depleted of its chemicals, or take an early retirement. Dad chose to leave and spent a few short years working for Bayer

Crop Science in Kansas City before he was pushed into retirement there. Having no strong ties to Kansas City, my parents moved once again, this time to Austin, Texas, to be closer to my sister and her family.

My dad and I talk infrequently on the phone—mainly, he just comments in the background when I am on the phone with my mom. We see each other twice a year, if we are lucky. The lack of regular interaction, the rapid way in which my father's sparse hair greys, his once-agile but now stiff body, and the involuntary yelp he emits when standing up or sitting down make each interaction feel increasingly fraught. I am not brave enough to start a conversation whose end I cannot foresee and whose impact I am certain will cause my father pain. My father chose us, our family, our future, over some external notion of ethics, in swearing allegiance to Carbide in 1984. At every juncture where chemicals have caused harm, he has chosen us again. Thus, I am indebted. I am implicated. My ethics, in the end, are not as dissimilar to his as I might wish them to be.

Even today, my dad reads the *Charleston Gazette* online each morning, scanning the obituaries for names of Carbiders he once worked with, then forwarding me the ones of those I knew and loved. He visits old colleagues in cities and towns where they have resettled all over the country. He remains the company man for a company that killed thousands and never fully owned up to the damage they caused. Union Carbide settled their lawsuits in India for a paltry $470 million—an average of less than $800 for each of the 592,000 people who filed claims. Warren Anderson, the chairman of the Union Carbide Corporation, a company once valued at over $10 billion, was declared a fugitive from justice by the Indian government and charged with manslaughter but was never extradited by the United States government. He died in 2014.

There is no Union Carbide Corporation left to hold responsible. There are no corporate bigwigs left with blood on their hands. There is only my Indian father, still storing Carbide jackets in his closet, and me, still using a thirty-year-old ice scraper emblazoned with the Carbide logo to remove ice from my windshield on winter mornings.

Nine Forms of the Goddess

🌱 🌿 🌱

⊚⊚⊚⊚⊚⊚

It is 1982, and nine Indian women have gathered in a circle in a basement in Cross Lanes, West Virginia, to celebrate the festival of Navratri. The basement floor is covered with bright-blue indoor/outdoor carpet, the walls are lined with honey-brown faux-wood paneling, and there is a red metal beam in the center of the room where a lighted brass pot called a garbo and idols of deities should typically stand. In sharp contrast to their damp surroundings, these women dress in their heaviest silk saris and best jewelry: finery brought with them in suitcases that travelled eight thousand miles from India to New York, sometimes by way of Kenya or Uganda or England, and then another five hundred miles from Jamaica, Queens, to the hills of West Virginia.

The women gather for as many of nine nights as they can spare each autumn. In Gujarati, *Nav* means "nine" and *rat* means "night." Each night, a different color inspires their clothing. Each night, a different incarnation of the goddess Durga is the focus of their worship. Durga, queen among Hindu goddesses, warrior for good, vanquisher of evil. She is often depicted astride a tiger, holding a sword, a trident, a mace, and a dagger in her many arms. *Durga* literally means "unassailable." The Mother goddess who will not be challenged or questioned in her battle to preserve the dharma of the righteous.

These worshippers of Durga begin each night the same way, singing the "Mataji Na Garba" in voices that are pitched and clear. With their words, they praise the many forms and powers of the Mother goddess. They slowly clap and slide around the circle, their motions repetitive and rhythmic. They pick up speed. The two-clap step gives way to a three-clap. Their bodies begin to blur, faces lost in a whirl of spin-ning, shining colors. The smell of sweat, mixing with that of perfume and powder, fills the room. In the morning, tiny purple bruises will dot their arms, elicited by the repeated banging of their glass bangles. The soles of their feet will bear the red marks of carpet burn. Their waists will host near-permanent indentations from the tightness of their petticoats. But for these nine nights, there is no pain insufferable enough to make them leave the circle early.

Nine women gather, nine nights, nine colors. Nine forms of the Mother goddess spinning in front of me.

Thirty-nine years later, I live in Boston and have no Indian community to speak of. There are weekend Navratri garbas in the suburbs, massive gatherings of Indians I do not know, in the gymnasiums of middle schools I've never heard of. I feel no pull to go to these anonymous celebrations, where ritual feels meaningless in the absence of relationships. Instead, the sharpest pang is the one asking me to go backwards in time, back to the tiny Indian community nestled in the Kanawha valley, back to the basement in Cross Lanes, back to the garba where the faces in the circle are the faces of my many mothers, and their characters are the unassailable personifications of Navadurga.

* * *

Though I was just three at the time, when I envision the Cross Lanes garba, I see myself as I look now, and my mothers are all my age. I take the place of Shailaputri, worshipped on the first day of Navratri. Like her, I, too, am a daughter of the mountains. Born and raised in West Virginia, I straddle the culture of my parents and the culture of my Appalachian birthplace. Autumn elicits nostalgia not just for Navratri but also for my home state, set aflame in oranges, yellows, and reds. I experience a double loss each fall, missing both the mountains of my childhood and the many mothers who played a role in raising me there. In Gujarati, the word for maternal aunt is *masi*—"mother-like." So it was that my mother's chosen sisters, cleaved to because of the familiarity they provided in the most foreign of contexts, became my masis. My mother-likes.

As the lone Indian girl in my classes at school, I was surrounded by White girls whose parents allowed them to dress in tight clothing, wear makeup, and put chemicals in their hair. Whether because of my awkward appearance, my brown skin, my yet-to-be-realized sexuality, or some combination of the three, dating was also never an option for me. I knew that I could not be like the girls in my classes, but struggled to build a cohesive identity for myself.

So it came to be that my many mothers took the traditional place of aunts and cousins in teaching me how to be a good woman and how to live a righteous life. In the absence of any other role models to help me understand what it meant to be an Indian woman, and what it meant to be in a relationship, their definitions are the ones I used to construct my own identity. Sometimes in a reflection of their image, and sometimes in direct opposition to it.

* * *

Dancing beside me in this ring of women is Asmita auntie, the mother of my oldest childhood friend. She embodies Brahmacharini, the incarnation of Durga best known for her devout austerity. For the entirety of my childhood, Asmita auntie lived in a one-level three-bedroom house with her husband and five children, on a single modest income earned at a job in West Virginia state government.

I invaded her house and refrigerator on a regular basis, sleeping over for multiple nights at a time and consuming every pickle in the jar, draining it of its neon brine afterwards. In retrospect, I can recognize the very real financial struggles her family faced. The ramen noodle lunches that felt like a guilty pleasure to me, when compared with my doctor-dad's demands that we eat fiber and salad, were a necessary staple in her feeding of five growing children. But she never once made me feel as though I was draining her wallet or that there wasn't room for me at her dark-brown laminate dining table.

Asmita auntie's house was the first place where I remember having conscious questions about gender in Indian culture. Auntie had four daughters and one son. Yet their car's license plate carried their son's name. So did the family business, even though her daughters were the ones earning honor roll, becoming valedictorians, and getting full scholarships to college. I never got the sense this was auntie's choice. But what did it mean about an Indian woman's ability to recognize and reward her daughters? To value and honor the lives they were creating instead of simply valuing a son for his maleness?

As I watched Asmita auntie's daughters rack up their awards, I wondered: What level of accomplishment would a woman need to ascend to in order for her success to outweigh her gender?

* * *

On my other side in the circle stands Alka auntie, exuding the peace and tranquility of Chandraghanta. Pale-skinned, with angular features and the most lilting of all the aunties' accents, Alka auntie showed her love for us through her cooking. I have never tasted a paneer dish in a restaurant, or in another home, that comes anywhere close to the perfect texture and seasoning of food I ate in her kitchen.

Even when I was young, I was cognizant of Alka auntie's grace and femininity—her perfectly coiffed hair, manicured nails, and beautifully tailored suits. Being around her heightened my awareness of my own frizzy hair, dark skin, bitten-down nails, and baggy clothes. I did not want to be like her; I simply saw in her a kind of womanhood I was certain I would never approximate.

What's more, she navigated the painful economic divides of her friendships with a kind of grace that blew me away as I got older and could see the potential for strain. While her friends bought increasingly bigger houses and fancier cars, Alka auntie's living conditions stayed the same. Yet my mom used to say that you could show up at Alka auntie's door at any time, on any day, and never feel anything but welcome. Job transitions, caring for aging parents, financial stressors—the weight of it all never showed on her face.

Alka auntie, who worked the hardest and died the youngest, of a lung cancer whose source we never understood. It was my many mothers who washed her body, combed her hair, trimmed her nails, did her makeup, and wrapped her in a sari for the final time before her cremation.

* * *

Next to Asmita auntie is the eldest of my mothers, and the elder in our community, Sudha auntie. She was one of the first handful of Indians to come to the Kanawha valley in the mid-sixties, forging the path for the hundred or so families who would eventually come to live in our community. Her husband, Stavan uncle, was killed in a terrible accident when his car was sideswiped as he pulled onto Big Tyler Road. Their children were barely teenagers at the time.

Sudha auntie was one of our community's first, and few, single mothers, and the living embodiment of Kushmanda, the deity who represents strength and courage in the face of adversity. She invited me to her house high on the hill of Mourning Dove for thalipeeth, a traditional Maharashtrian dish, every time I came home from college. And no matter how badly her arthritic hands ached or how hard her fingers fought to return to their clenched-fist state, she refused to let me help her pat the dough into shape or fry it on the skillet.

"You sit and rest," she would say. "You work so hard in school. The least I can do is feed you."

In a culture where the quantity of ghee used is equated with the quantity of love felt, Sudha auntie's thalipeeth always arrived at the table with innumerable pools of clarified butter glistening on its crispy surface.

* * *

Sudha auntie's neighbor, both in the circle and in our town of Cross Lanes, is Jyotsana auntie. Her enthusiasm for garba, and the grace with which she moves around the garbo, is unmatched. The shortest of all the women, with a braid that runs half the length of her body, she makes up for in energy what she lacks in height. She is Skanda Mata incarnate— pure and divine of nature. The most religiously devout of my mothers, Jyotsana auntie is the person to ask when questions of ritual or faith arise. She is also a walking Gujarati dictionary and the sunniest person I know.

When I took my White, Jewish/Irish/Italian female partner to West Virginia to meet my mothers and sent a hesitant text to each one asking if they wanted to meet us, this was the rejoinder that she and her husband, Prakash uncle, sent:

> Neema, I am angry with you that you felt the need to call and ask if we are ok with your and Laura's visit. We are your second home and family. So no matter what, we will always be there for you. Also don't waste your money by staying in a hotel or some other place. We have plenty of rooms (may not be as clean) and save money for the gas (went up yesterday by 40 cents per gallon). See you soon.

Their words were catharsis, followed by actions that further confirmed a fact I should have known all along: that for my mothers, love dampened any prejudices that might have occurred to them otherwise.

Jyotsana auntie embraced Laura and called her beta (my child), much as she did for all of the young people in our community. After meeting us in a restaurant for dinner, she insisted that we come to her house and sit in her living room, where she plied us with slices of mango pie and cups of chai. There was no judgment in her heart, only a kind of unconditional love and acceptance that I am blessed to have bestowed upon me.

* * *

The owner of the basement where this garba unfolds, Ranjana auntie, makes her way around the circle beside Jyotsana auntie. She is a living manifestation of Katyayani, who is described as having wild hair and eighteen arms, and emitting a radiant light from her body that makes it impossible for darkness and evil to hide. Ranjana auntie is tall, with untamed curly hair and a Cindy Crawford mole above her lip. She is by far the most disciplinarian of my mothers.

I simultaneously feared Ranjana auntie and was awed by her. Her magical sitting room, with its zebra-skin wall hangings, orange plush birdcage chair, and cinema organ, was so different from the staid furniture in my own house, and in those of my neighbors. Her kitchen almost always had a caged bird in it that would utter random Gujarati phrases when you walked in.

Once, my parents left me in her care when they went out of town. During our time together, she decided to take me to Sears for a photo shoot. Ranjana auntie styled my long, curly hair in a fashion far different from my traditional braid. She dressed me in cute jeans, a fitted red Sesame Street turtle-neck, and cowboy boots, and coaxed me into a pose where I am sitting with one leg crossed over the other, laughing almost flirtatiously.

It is the most *girly* photo in my album of pictures from childhood, somehow managing to be more feminine than all of my awkward prom pictures combined. She didn't ask my parents for permission to take these photos beforehand, just gave them the prints afterwards. Proof, perhaps, that my tomboy self could be tamed if they took it upon themselves to do the taming, as she had.

Ranjana auntie lost her pain-filled battle with oral cancer before I could ask her the questions I now have about her childhood in Tanzania, about being a working mom when so many of her peers were staying at home, about being un-afraid to live her life in the boldest of reds, greens, and yellows even as those around her continually tried to tone her down.

* * *

Next to Ranjana auntie is my mother's best friend in this group, Manju auntie. Her garba style is stiffer than that of her neighbors in the circle. Garba is not Manju auntie's strong suit in the way that it is for some of the other women, but she participates nonetheless. The mother of three sons, Manju auntie has called my sister and me her daughters from the outset. We benefit from all her motherly love, with none of the filial responsibility.

She fills yoghurt containers with enough fried snacks to last me for weeks after a visit, insists that I eat a meal with her at her home high in the hills that ring the city of Charleston, and cooks my favorite foods, most especially her okra, which is crispy in a way I am never able to replicate. Manju auntie was the first person my mom called when I came out to her, and she embraced Laura with the no-nonsense logic that she applies to all situations.

"If Neema is happy, and Laura makes her happy, that is what matters to me," she told my mom. When my mom has struggled with reconciling my identity with the beliefs of her traditional Indian family, it is Manju auntie who has counseled her, firmly stating that those family members need to "figure it out and deal with it," and that it isn't my job, or my mom's, to accommodate them.

Though she has always been consistent with me, Manju auntie's personality is much like that of Kaal Ratri, the goddess who is both honored and feared. She runs hot and cold in a way that can be unpredictable. I watched my mom's friendship with Manju auntie ebb and flow over the years, and learned from their interactions how to navigate the changing terrain of friendship, how to provide space without running away.

* * *

To Manju auntie's right in the circle, my sister Swati dances with abandon, her heavy sari no match for her love of dancing. Her eyes are bright and lined with kajol; her long black hair spills down her back. Seven years older than me, born when my mother was just twenty-one, Swati has always inhabited complex space in our family: sometimes closer to a sister than a daughter for my mom, and sometimes closer to a mother than a sister for me.

Swati is the voice of calm and reason in this group, the goddess Maha Gauri, whose primary power is her ability to allay fears. When I decided to start telling my family about Laura—the only relationship I've ever shared with them—there was no doubt in my mind that Swati was the person to tell first.

I called her one summer evening in 2010 from the parking lot of Roxbury Community College, where I was attending a teacher training. Words spilled out in a rush, some combination of "I'm dating a woman," "It's serious," and "Please don't tell mom and dad yet."

There was no hesitation in Swati's voice when she finally got a chance to speak. "I'm so happy for you, Neema. I can't wait to meet her."

It was Swati who coached me through how to tell my mom about Laura. It is Swati who has held every debrief conversation with my mom when she hasn't understood my choices: why, for example, I won't attend a wedding when Laura's name isn't written on the invitation. Or why I don't want to visit India after hearing homophobic comments from family members on my last visit.

And it is Swati who now helps me navigate new terrain: that of trying to become a mother myself, in a way that none of my many mothers was able to model for me. On this rocky path of sperm donors, failed inseminations, bottomed-out FSH numbers, a decision to switch which partner carries, and attempting pregnancy during a pandemic—her constancy and calm have sometimes been the only trail markers signaling a way forward.

* * *

The last person in this tight circle of fabric and flesh is my own mother, her smiling face ringed by wisps of hair that have escaped from her tight braid. She is the one whose singing voice I hear most clearly, because it is the voice that never falters during garba. Her grace and femininity are traits I have come to appreciate over the years, even as I've come to accept that they have been passed on to my sister and niece, and have skipped me. Acceptance of this fact has not come as easily for her.

When I was small, my mom would sing the same bedtime songs to me that her brother had sung to her when she was growing up. One, in particular, stands out in my mind. It was a song about a single woman who doesn't understand why she is still single. Each verse outlines all the qualities that make her a desirable bride. Her father has a car, her grandfather has a horse and buggy, her uncle has a flower garden. She is fairer than her older sister and skinnier than her younger sister. She goes to college, goes out to eat in restaurants, and goes to see movies. And yet, despite all this, she remains single.

My mom took the song's message at face value: the role of a woman in India was to marry, bear children, and be an obedient wife and giving mother. She has spent the last fifty years performing those gendered expectations to the best of her ability, marrying my father after just a few short months of knowing him, raising children with him, growing old with him. I listened to the same song and thought, in the words of any typical six-year-old, "What kind of capitalist, sexist, shadist nonsense is this?" Our paths in life have been quite different as a result.

In this group of women, my mother is the peacemaker and the relationship builder. When she moved away from the Kanawha valley after thirty years of living there, the ties among the rest of the women slowly unraveled. My mother is Siddhidatri, the giver of supernatural powers. She constantly seeks out learning opportunities and ways to share her experiences with those around her. More than any of her peers, she threw herself into the broader American community of Charleston, West Virginia. She did taxes for free at the local library for the working-class White folks who needed help completing their paperwork. She volunteered as a docent in our tiny art museum. She became the leader of my Girl Scout troop and used the opportunity to educate my White peers about Indian culture and customs. She earned her MBA at night, then got her CPA, and worked fifteen-hour days during tax season but never failed to have dinner on the table at night for her family. And she did all of this while negotiating the impossible demands and expectations of a traditional Indian man and entitled children.

I told my mom I was dating Laura when we were sitting at her dinner table late one night in Kansas City. I was crying as I told her, uncertain as to what her response would be.

"The most important thing to me is that you are happy, Neema. I just don't want your life to be any harder than it has to be, and I worry that this will make it harder."

For a woman who was raised in a country where being gay was illegal until September of 2018, and who spent the majority of her adulthood in the Bible Belt, this response was more than I could have asked for. But her subsequent response, her embrace of Laura, the mushy letters she sends her each birthday saying, "I'm so happy that Neema has you in her life," have proved yet again that my mom's capacity for growth, and for love, is boundless.

I was not fair to my mom growing up, unable to recognize the impossible balancing act she accomplished every day as she advanced in her education and career and still put a traditional Gujarati dinner, with its four separately prepared components, on the table each night. I still cringe remembering the moment as a teenager when I yelled at my mom because a piece of clothing I needed hadn't yet been ironed. As an adult, struggling to work, take care of my home, be present in my relationship, and be an engaged aunt for my niece, I wish for my mom to bestow me with the supernatural powers she seems to possess.

* * *

Today is Dussehra, the tenth day of Navratri. After nine days of fasting, feasting, and dancing, Navratri in India ends with this tenth day off from work and school to celebrate the victory of good over evil. Effigies of demons get burnt in bonfires. People begin new jobs and new journeys.

In Boston this Dussehra, the sky is grey and it is raining. Laura's Irish-Italian father is here for a visit, and we will spend the day together carbo-loading: starting with breakfast at a diner, followed by a beer tasting where I politely endure bitter sips of brew, and ending with three courses of pasta for dinner. It is quite possibly the least Indian of Navratri experiences that my mothers could have wished for me. Still, I know they would be proud that I am doing what they taught me to do: be family in the way that people need you to be. And though I can't stand in circle with them this Navratri, it is their faces, their voices, their presence that I feel when the first sounds of the garba come through my speakers on my drive home from work. It is them I seek to honor when I sing praises to Durga Mata, the Mother goddess.

Be Like Wilt

⚘ ⚘ ⚘

⊙⊙⊙⊙⊙⊙

I stand on the foul line at the Cross Lanes Methodist Church gym. I am nine, the only girl playing on an all-boys basketball team. The only Brown kid on a team of White boys, my puny arms, thick glasses, and long, oiled braid set me even further apart from their wiry, muscular bodies and cropped blond haircuts.

Why has Carl Bradford chosen me for his team? I wonder about this. His sons are two of the quickest, highest-scoring players in our local league. In 1988 in Cross Lanes, West Virginia, there is no designated league for girls, and when I try out one Saturday in October, there are only two other girls in the gym with close to eighty boys.

"Tryouts," in this pre-hypercompetitive era, involve dribbling up and down the court and shooting two layups and a couple of foul shots. Every kid is guaranteed a space on a team. The question is simply which coach will choose to take them on.

Each girl is selected for a different team. Some teams have no girls. Mr. Bradford doesn't have to pick me, but he does anyway. In doing so, he also takes on the responsibility of chauffeuring me to and from practices and games. Basketball is not a sport my immigrant parents understand, and the parental time commitment it requires is not something their lives leave space for. By opting to play, I take a step further away from my nuclear family and closer to my West Virginia community.

Still, my Indian genetics make me short, weak, and terribly uncoordinated. When I shoot the ball overhand, it falls short of the basket by several feet. When I play defense, my teammates say I look like a praying mantis, my hands weaving in front of me instead of out to the sides. I love the game, but I am about as far from a natural talent as my parents' hometown in India is from this gym at the end of Frontier Drive.

One evening, Mr. Bradford proposes that I shoot the ball a different way. Not overhand, as I've been trying to, but underhand. "Granny-style," my teammates disparagingly call it.

"Some of the greatest basketball players of all time shot underhand, Neema," Mr. Bradford says. "Wilt Chamberlain shot underhand." His blue eyes, magnified by round, wire-rimmed glasses, probe mine.

In my adult life, I have listened to entire podcasts about the accuracy of the granny shot, about how Wilt Chamberlain scored one hundred points in the one game where he shot free throws underhand, and Rick Barry's career free-throw percentage was a chart-topping 89.3 because he opted to do the same. But at age nine, I feel like this is yet another way in which I am being set apart from my peers. Raised by fathers who were players of the game, taught to play at driveway hoops as soon as they could walk, they can shoot overhand. I cannot.

How do you assimilate into the dominant culture when your own culture is so invisible to the majority? My small group of Indian peers and I answer this question in different ways. The only Indian boy at my elementary school, who all of the White kids either think is my brother or insist I should date, speaks with an exaggerated twang, drinks heavily through high school, and loudly votes Republican later on. Some of the Indian kids who live in the city of Charleston emulate their wealthy White classmates, picking up tennis or golf as entry points into American culture.

As for me, I choose basketball. I play the sport constantly, watch it obsessively on the TV in our basement, and rock my satin turquoise-and-purple Charlotte Hornets jacket daily, and not simply because I love the game. I do, but basketball is more than just a sport to me. It is my way into a world where I otherwise don't seem to belong.

I blush hard at the suggestion to shoot underhand, dribble a basketball against the white linoleum flooring of the gym, and stare at the black curve of the key instead of making eye contact with Mr. Bradford. I know he is right, but am not sure I can find the courage to shoot granny-style in a game where all of my teammates and classmates from school will be watching.

Much later in his career, Chamberlain explained why he only shot underhand for one season and reverted to the less accurate overhand free throw afterward.

"I felt silly, like a sissy, shooting underhanded," he said. "I know I was wrong. I know some of the best foul shooters in history shot that way. I just couldn't do it." Even though I haven't heard this explanation in 1988, I struggle with the same sentiment.

Eventually, however, my desire to make a basket overwhelms my fear of judgment. Game day comes, the point guard gets the ball into my hands, and I position the ball between my legs before hurling it upwards.

Swish.

It isn't a buzzer-beater. It's not the game-winning shot. It is just two points scored midway through the third quarter in a regular-season game. But the entire gym erupts in cheers, the crowd chanting my name. Someone even calls my mom from the pay phone in the corner. I grow so dizzy with this temporary but overwhelming sense of belonging that I fail to register the final score.

After the game, Mr. Bradford gives me his slow, sweet smile.

"See, Neema? It doesn't matter *how* you shoot the ball. It just matters that the ball goes in."

Mr. Bradford drafts me for his team each of the next three years. At the end of my last season, he persuades all the coaches to jointly award me the league's "Heart and Hustle" trophy, given not to the most talented player but to the most dedicated team member. It remains, to this day, the award I cherish most. When I age out of his league, he recruits me as an assistant coach for his younger son's team. His red Jeep Cherokee is a fixture outside our house at least three days a week, as he continues to drive me to and from practices and games.

Each evening after practice, we drive over Goff Mountain. The headlights of the Jeep cast the only light on the dark and winding road that takes us past a pungent chemical landfill and through a dense stand of trees.

"Close your eyes now," he commands as we approach the summit of the mountain.

In the backseat, the boys and I giggle and grin, close our eyes, take a deep breath. Mr. Bradford hits the gas, and we soar over the first hill, our stomachs dropping, roller-coaster style. The Jeep bounces hard onto the concrete, then takes flight again as we hit the second decline.

For this brief moment, we are Bo, Luke, and Daisy in the General Lee. Our screams of delight replace the sounds of "Dixie" in this reimagined Dukes of Hazzard, and I am wildly, freely *American* in a way I can never recapture outside of Mr. Bradford's presence.

○○○○○○

The Blue-Red Divide

🌱 🌿 🌱

○○○○○○

Before Mrs. B got sick with cancer, before Hillary Clinton went to West Virginia and announced, "Coal is not coming back," before our hometown earned the awful nickname "Needle City," and before my blue-from-birth home state went 80 percent red in the 2016 election, Mr. B's Facebook posts were about one of two topics: riverboats or Christianity.

As a general rule, I "❤️ed" the riverboats and skipped right over the gospel music. Riverboats symbolize a part of our shared past: Mr. B served in the navy during World War II, and his love of boats tracks back to his time in the service. So deep was his love, in fact, that he decorated their living room with a nautical theme, the mantel peppered with ship's instruments, the walls dotted with nautical charts. The Bs even owned a coffee table made with a wooden ship wheel overlaid by heavy glass.

My Indian immigrant parents, who looked to the Bs as guides when assimilating into White West Virginian culture in the late 1970s, chose to emulate that element of home decor when they furnished our house. A nod to their adopted parents' nautical past, fused with elements of their Indian one.

Mr. B's affinity for locks and dams and riverboats inspired

the Avashia family to go to the Sternwheel Regatta in down-town Charleston every summer: a race where wooden boats painted white and red puttered down the Kanawha River on paddle wheels. When we visited the B's house high up on a hill in South Charleston, a black-and-white painted buoy guarded the entrance to the house. On our visits, I stood in awe of the giant ship wheel mounted on the wall of their wood-paneled rec room, which Mrs. B jokingly called Mr. B's "*wreck* room." Much later in my life, when I found myself on the banks of the Mississippi for the first time in Vicks-burg, I called Mr. B and described its muddy expanse to him. He had always wanted to take a cruise up the Mississippi; I tried to take him on one vicariously.

Mr. B's boat posts on Facebook evoke sweet memories of my childhood. They remind me of growing up in a river valley dotted with chemical plants like Union Carbide, where my dad and Mr. B worked together, and where they struck up the unlikeliest of friendships in the mid-1970s: my dark-haired, brown-skinned father, the nerdy new plant doctor, and Mr. B, a high school–educated engineer nearly twenty years senior, born and bred in the hills of West Virginia. To listen to a con-versation between the two was an exercise in sociolinguistics, my father incorporating elements of Mr. B's southern accent into his own Indian-English patter, Mr. B modulating his thick accent to make sure my dad could keep up.

Our family came to the Kanawha valley in one of the ear-liest wavelets of Indian immigrants after the passage of the 1965 Hart-Celler Act, which eased restrictions on immigra-tion from Asia. A small cohort of those Indians travelled to West Virginia to work in chemicals, coal, and the associated healthcare that such deadly work required. Demographically, Indians have made up less than 0.5 percent of the popula-tion for their entire time living in the state. Outside of Native Americans, they are the smallest statistical minority in a state whose total non-White population has never exceeded 5 percent.

It was customary, at the time of my family's arrival in 1973, for folks at the plant to invite the new doc and his family over for dinner. But my foreign family posed a conundrum. What should one cook for strict vegetarians? The previous plant doctor, and the one before him, and the one before him had all been White. American. Well versed in the West Virginia staples of pinto beans and cornbread, in dinner plates that always consisted of a meat, a starch, and, occasionally, an overboiled vegetable. People had no schema for what a vegetarian meal should even look like.

Mrs. B told me this story shortly before she died. After three full decades of looking no older than sixty, she suddenly seemed incredibly frail on my visit in June of 2017. The softness vanished from her body, the creaminess from her skin. The cancerous growths on her lungs gained ground, making it so difficult for her to breathe that she no longer left the house. Not even for church on Sundays.

Sensing this visit would most likely be our last, I asked how our families came to break bread together so regularly, with the Bs coming over to try Indian food and my mother making forays into other cuisines, and us going to their house for calico casserole (mixed vegetables and cream of mushroom soup baked with a Ritz cracker topping), roasted potatoes, and green salad with Italian dressing.

"No one else knew what to cook for your mom and dad. And I just figured, why not just make all of the side dishes and leave out the meat?" she told me.

And cook she did, serving us dinners on delicate china once a month for the entirety of my childhood. Even after I went away to college, then graduate school, then life as a middle school teacher in Boston, she insisted that I come over for dinner on every visit home. Well into her mid-eighties, she would get out her blender and bread maker and whip up a creamy, dilly zucchini bisque and warm bread when I stopped by. Or fry up a batch of green tomatoes. Or, close to the end, make me drink her perfectly sweetened sweet tea out of a heavy, cut glass tumbler. The intersection of food and love was one that my Indian family and the Bs' West Virginian one both understood intuitively.

Mrs. B cooked, Mr. B repaired. If any appliance in our house went kaput, Mr. B showed up within the hour, in faded blue jeans and a white T-shirt, a bandanna tied around his forehead to keep his thick, grey-brown bangs out of his face. He assessed the situation and headed back to his truck for the tools needed to make the repair. And then he tinkered and perspired and wrestled with the machine until he got it to comply, my dad standing alongside, the apprentice watching the appliance wizard at work.

In turn, my father became the Bs' unofficial family doctor. He served as consult on every medical decision, including Mrs. B's decision to refuse chemotherapy upon diagnosis of a slow-growing tumor on her lung, with an estimated twelve-month life expectancy. On trips to India, he purchased the blood pressure medicines they needed in bulk, the cost in rupees being so much cheaper than the prescription drug copay on Carbide health insurance for retirees.

"Wasn't that unethical?" my partner Laura once asked me. I couldn't find the words to explain that "ethical" means something different when it comes to people you love. Or that ethics don't apply in the same way when you are a company doctor in a company town. Maybe they should. But they don't.

Even after my parents moved away from Charleston in 2003, first to Kansas City and then to Austin, the weekly phone consults with "Doc" continued. The relationship, as I saw it, was truly reciprocal, both in the abstractions of love and in the concreteness of service. For that reason, even seventeen years after my parents' departure from West Virginia, I have returned to Charleston each year, largely for one purpose: to see the Bs. They are home to me. Without them, I feel unrooted.

I imagine Mr. B keeping the death watch all those months after Mrs. B decided not to continue treatment and instead to let her cancer take its course. How difficult it must have been to watch his partner of seventy years fade away. How my father's step-by-step explanation of cancer's progression, gently rendered in the rec room on their farewell visit, must have run through his mind: first the coughing and shortness of breath, then the spatters of blood, and ultimately the rupture and bleed-out when the tumor perforated the lung.

The time stamps on his Facebook posts indicate as much, peppered with anxious 3 a.m. wake-ups that only seem to have increased in the months after her death. The ratio has shifted, too, with fewer posts about riverboats and gospel, bringing the newsfeed closer to that of an anti-immigrant, anti-woman, anti–Black Lives Matter Trump voter. Just recently, I logged in to Facebook to find an upsetting post about undocumented immigration.

Heaven has a Wall and strict immigration policies. Hell has open borders.

Let that sink in.

I called my mom to ask her about it. "Mom, have you seen Mr. B's posts? I don't know what to do. They are so painful to look at."

The palpable resignation in her response made me even sadder. "What can we do, Neema? It's the same thing with so many people from West Virginia. The only thing we can do is not talk politics." I am the child of immigrants. My parents are the immigrants themselves. If Mr. B's Facebook posts feel like arrows to me, it would seem they are daggers for my parents. Daggers they ignore because of the debt of gratitude they feel; because of the heavy burden that accompanies four-and-a-half decades of love.

"Not talking politics" was the West Virginia way growing up. Sometimes I question whether I just wasn't paying attention or whether this was actually the case, but when I look around my Massachusetts neighborhood at the political signs that pop up on lawns, at the bumper stickers on the back of every car, I am convinced it is true. Even on a recent visit back to West Virginia, in the depths of the Trump era, the lawn sign game was minor league compared to Massachusetts'. People truly didn't advertise their political affiliations. I never knew how my neighbors voted, and West Virginia was so dark blue for most of my childhood that I never really thought to ask the question. Maybe the Bs were conservatives all along, and I just never knew it. Or maybe, as I've tried to justify it to my judgmental, liberal New England friends, the destruction wrought by joblessness and rampant opioid addiction on my home state has created a kind of helpless rage that is only stoked by the xenophobic rhetoric.

I scour Mr. B's Facebook page sometimes, trying my hardest to make meaning out of the misery his posts evoke in me. The only other photos he occasionally posts are of a Charleston long gone. One where Capitol Street was full of thriving shops, Stone & Thomas department store was always busy, and a steady stream of coal- and chemical-laden boats and barges traversed the Kanawha. One where our town possessed a healthy, growing middle class, and you could make a solid living by earning a high school diploma, working thirty years at the plant, then retiring with full benefits and pension at age fifty-five. One that, in truth, hasn't existed since the mid-1980s.

The chemical industry in the valley died a slow, painful death after Union Carbide's Bhopal leak in 1984, known to be the largest chemical disaster in human history. Each subsequent year brought more pink slips, more abandoned production units. As chemicals went, so too did coal. Hillary Clinton's campaign message to miners was harsh but true. Coal isn't coming back. China has cornered the market. Simply put, there is no industry to hold up West Virginia's economy. Walmart is now the state's largest employer. The only other state I've visited where the poverty feels on par with that of my home state is Mississippi. A drive through the most struggling parts of either will leave you dizzy with despair.

In this way, there is an authenticity to Mr. B's longing for a time when things were "great": when he was young, his family thriving, all of them living lives full of purpose and meaning in a town that was significantly more economically healthy than the one he sees now, full of shuttered stores, heroin needles littering the pavement out front. Modern American prosperity has eluded much of West Virginia. This is not up for debate.

Right-wing politicians' threats do not negate Mr. B's existence in the way they negate mine or my family's. What's more, their promises resonate for Mr. B in a way that they don't for me—queer, Brown, and living in liberal, economically healthy Massachusetts. Ultimately, our politics are profoundly personal, our worldview refined through the lens of our own experiences. It can be hard to hold on to this under-standing of Mr. B in moments of frustration, and moments of fear, but I am trying hard to do so.

Growing up, only a few members of our extended family lived in the United States: My mom's older brother in Akron, Ohio. My dad's younger brother in Champaign, Illinois. And my mom's nephew in Tampa, Florida. We were lucky to see each other even twice a year. "Family" and, in particular, "grandparents" were concepts I knew were important be-cause I watched my friends and neighbors spend every week-end and every holiday with theirs. But what could an Indian kid in West Virginia do when so much of her blood family lived so damn far away and the ones who lived closer were immigrants working nonstop in pursuit of the much-touted American Dream?

I improvised. Put the feelings that normally would have been directed at blood relatives onto my West Virginian neighbors, who became my adoptive aunts and uncles. Took the love usually reserved for grandparents and directed it, full throttle, at the Bs. I referred to them as my grandparents in my mind, and sometimes even out loud in conversation with non–West Virginians, trying to explain the depth of the relationship.

Shortly before President Obama was elected in 2008, I vis-ited the Bs and found myself in a conversation about race in West Virginia. I wasn't yet thirty, so perhaps can be forgiven for thoughtlessly stumbling into a patch of stinging nettles. I shared with the Bs that West Virginia's overwhelmingly nega-tive response to the Obama candidacy had been hard for me, and had unearthed a number of previously buried challeng-ing childhood experiences with racism. The Bs' kindness to-wards our family hadn't been mirrored by some of my peers in school, who wore Confederate flags with pride and took ample opportunities to spit on, slap, or shower me with slurs.

Mrs. B looked at me with her clear blue eyes and said, with genuine innocence in her voice, "You know, it's funny. I never really saw color when I looked at you all. I just saw you, and loved you."

Twenty-nine-year-old Neema accepted this statement as fact. As an expression of love, rooted in color-blindness though it may have been. Forty-two-year-old Neema, post-Obama backlash, post–Oak Creek Sikh temple massacre, post-2016 election, post–White supremacist killing of Srinivas Kuchibhotla, post-2021 siege on the Capitol by Proud Boys and QAnon followers, is full of questions about what this meant about our relationship all along. Maybe we didn't talk politics, but that doesn't mean I didn't *feel* political. Was my family only acceptable because we were viewed as an exception? Would we have been experienced differently, embraced less quickly, if my parents hadn't assimilated so willingly? Is minority presence in a community only acceptable when we make up less than 1 percent of the overall population?

In the years between thirty and forty-two, my questions about our relationship have only grown more complicated. Each time I visited West Virginia with Laura, I left her behind when I visited the Bs. She drank cups of lukewarm coffee at Tim Hortons, wandered around our dilapidated mall, or made repeated trips up and down the aisles of the local Walmart, while I sat on the floral print sofa in the Bs' living room, chatting and sipping sweet tea.

Just as I struggled to share my relationship with my conservative Indian family members, I struggled to test my decades-old relationship with my adopted grandparents by introducing them to Laura. I don't remember a time when the Bs didn't attend the Bible Center Church out Corridor G at least twice a week. They played a huge role in the construction of a new building at the site. They sometimes spoke of moving into the retirement community being constructed by the church at a later point. And the gospel posts on Mr. B's Facebook page replayed in my mind on repeat. When Laura finally met the Bs on our last visit to Charleston, primarily because I needed her to know Mrs. B before I lost her to cancer, she came as my friend, not my partner. I shielded them still, not wanting my identity, my relationship, to be a source of discomfort for them.

Only now do I wonder, Does Mr. B ever think to shield me?

But I also have to ask hard questions of myself. What benefit did shielding the Bs from the truth about my love life confer? Would our relationship now be less vulnerable if I had been more honest along the way? Or would it have shattered long ago? I want to believe that the Bs' love was unconditional; it is only Mr. B's Facebook posts that have sowed the seeds of doubt.

After Mrs. B's death, my parents donated money to create a children's playroom at the Kanawha Valley Hospice, which cared for her until the end. They wanted to make a space for the children and grandchildren who visit their family members in hospice and need a place to decompress and play while there. They requested the room be named in Mrs. B's honor. In India, when a parent dies, this is the custom among people who can afford to do so: You create a lasting tribute that benefits the larger community. You name it after the loved one who has died. My parents dedicated school rooms and hospital wards in India when their biological parents died. The playroom was their way of declaring to the world, I think, that Mrs. B had been a second mother to them both.

My dad asked me to write the inscription for the plaque outside the door to the playroom. "In loving memory of Mrs. B," it reads. "Every room she entered was filled with warmth and joy. Every person she met was better for having known her."

Her daughter-in-law mailed me a thank-you card in response. "I hope you know that she considered you all family just as much as she did her other children and grandchildren," she wrote.

Every thirty days, Facebook "unsnoozes" Mr. B, and I am reminded of our fissures by another post that challenges some aspect of my identity. The most recent one was a screed against the children of undocumented immigrants.

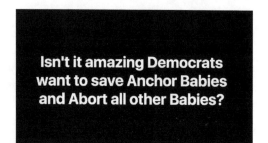

Isn't it amazing Democrats want to save Anchor Babies and Abort all other Babies?

My sister, presumably, was an "anchor baby" at birth, born to parents who were not yet citizens. Does he think of her when he reposts the hatred spewed by Russian bots and Proud Boys? When he declares his support of a president and political party who have successfully turned "immigration" into a swear word and made people like my parents, and like my students, the scapegoats responsible for America's demise?

Does he think of us, or of his daughters and granddaughters, when he posts images like the one he shared during the Kavanaugh hearings trivializing the accusations of sexual assault leveled against the nominee?

Mr. B is the kind of father, grandfather, and great-grandfather who loves so fully, it is hard to imagine him responding to the attack of someone he loves in this way. Does he know and dissociate? Or does he just live in denial that one in five women and one in seventy-one men will be raped in their

I'M SO SORRY THAT BAD MAN TOUCHED YOU INAPPROPRIATELY

LET'S WAIT 30 OR 40 YEARS... UNTIL HE RUNS FOR OFFICE... AGAINST A DEMOCRAT!

lifetimes? Some, undoubtedly, by past, present, and future Supreme Court justices. Still, I don't engage. I hover over the like button, note that the same three people have liked every single one of his inflammatory posts. Not even one of them is a member of his family. I keep it moving after that. If they can hold their tongues, so must I.

In 2018, the *Atlantic* ran an article about a Pew Research Center study measuring people's ability to discern fact from opinion based on age. From a list of five facts and five opinions, only 17 percent of those over age sixty-five successfully identified all five facts correctly.

I thought of Mr. B as I read this study. Wondered how his aging mind, five years past ninety, processes the rapid-fire misinformation that social media bombards us with.

Especially when combined with having so much more free time on his hands since Mrs. B's passing. I tried to find a reason, yet again, to push the morning's posted hateful memes out of my mind, and focus on the sweetness of going with him to a Charleston Wheelers minor league baseball game when I was eleven. Of eating green beans fresh from his garden. Of discussing a strategic approach to dishwasher repair and then being able to rejoice with him when I'd successfully fixed mine. Of the firm hug and "I love you" I get every time we say goodbye.

The posts continue, and each time one comes across my feed, I flinch, then force myself to look away. Each time, I start to respond, then quickly delete my words before I can post them. Each time, I conjure a honeyed childhood memory to counter the sting of his present-day beliefs. And when the posts become too unbearable, I turn to my mom's advice: to not talk politics with loving people whose politics have become so profoundly disparate from my own. I simply click on the three little dots in the top right corner of his latest provocative post and select "Snooze for 30 days." I won't unfollow. I won't unfriend. I snooze and hope for a time when my only living grandfather and I can find a way to see each other fully once again.

City Mouse/Country Mouse

✿ ✿ ✿

◎◎◎◎◎

My partner of eleven years, Laura, grew up in Brooklyn long before Brooklyn became bougie. Her neighborhood of Kensington is probably one of just a handful in Brooklyn where you can still feel its working-class, immigrant roots even today. The bodegas are still bodegas, not organic food co-ops. The main drag is dotted with Bangladeshi and Russian grocery stores and outposts for Yummy Taco instead of vegan ice cream shops and yoga studios. Her New York, the one she remembers growing up in, is the one that existed prior to Giuliani's police-enforced gentrification.

And in that gritty, unbougie, beloved New York, she was taught by her mother, very firmly, not to talk to strangers. Not to make eye contact with people on the train. To set her face into a stern, bordering on frown, position when in public. To inherently be suspicious of anyone approaching her, asking for anything.

Which is why, the first time I saw Laura in 2008, with her "don't fuck with me" face, dangling earrings, and neck swathed in a scarf, I thought to myself, "This woman is both beautiful and potentially mean." The complete opposite of my bumpkin self: happiest in flannel shirts and ratty blue jeans, with a face so open that complete strangers always, always approach me to ask for help, and a dogged determination to greet everyone I see on the streets of Boston as I pass, even if they pretend I'm invisible most of the time. Though I have lived outside of the South for more years than I lived in it at this point, the manners bred into me early have persisted, just as New York manners have for Laura.

We are an interracial, same-sex, trans-Mason-Dixon-line couple. Which makes us quite the complicated pair.

* * *

Among all of Aesop's fables, the one I loved most as a child was the one about the city mouse and the country mouse, two cousins who have grown up in vastly different circumstances. When the city mouse goes to the country, he is wildly disappointed by his cousin's simple life, and dismissive of the wholesome, farm-to-table meal his cousin serves. He demands that the country mouse come to visit him and experience the opulence of the city. Together, they dine at a fancy city restaurant, and the country mouse is almost, almost convinced that the city mouse has it right, when suddenly their meal is interrupted by snarling dogs, forcing them to abandon their dinner and flee. The country mouse decides that city living is not for him, declaring, "I'd rather gnaw on a bean than be gnawed by continual fear."

Never ever, when reading that story, did it occur to me that I would decide to spend my life with a city mouse. Even later in life, when it became clear to me that I could not go back to West Virginia after four years of college in Pittsburgh—that I had tasted the sumptuousness of the city and was willing to risk the snarling dogs—I always thought, on some level, I would end up with someone who shared an impossibly similar, desi-fied, countrified background. Someone who grew up with an appreciation for moving slowly, sitting on porches for hours without purpose, savoring every drop in a cold glass of sweet tea. And to be totally honest, I'd also always imagined that person would be an Indian man.

For the first eight years out of school, that's what I tried to look for. "The needle in the haystack" project, I called it to my friends, who protested that my criteria were too narrow and that I was closing myself off to potentially amazing relationships because of that constricted view. And they were right. Between ages eighteen and thirty, I rarely got past date #3 with any one person. And then I turned thirty, and I looked at the life I'd created for myself, both what I loved about it and what I lacked, and I realized that the tight set of rules and patterns I'd locked myself into—only Indian men, preferably southern ones—was wholly unfulfilling.

What was the point of all these limitations if they weren't helping me get closer to the life I wanted to be living?

The year of thirty, I decided, would be the year of breaking patterns. No more setting narrow parameters for whom I would date, no more Indiandating.com, no more saying no.

The year of thirty, as it turned out, was the year I met Laura, who shattered every parameter I'd ever constructed.

* * *

A teacher meet-cute in five scenes:

Two eighth-grade teachers are drawn to an announcement for a working group forming to address the challenges eighth graders in Boston face in the transition to high school. We meet one evening in the waning months of 2008 in a local coffee shop and sit at opposite ends of the table from one another, noticing each other, but just barely.

Then, we run into each other again at a Saturday afternoon showing of *The Class* in March at the Coolidge Corner Theatre.

Then again walking along the Southwest Corridor on the

first weekend in May, when Jamaica Plain's Wake Up the Earth festival is in full swing.

Our work on the transition-to-high-school project picks up. We email and chat online and plan for a presentation to the mayor. By fall, we are spending time together on weekends. At Thanksgiving, I give Laura a ride to Brooklyn on my way to my cousin's house in central Jersey. "It's on the way," I tell her, even though it is clearly not. We stop to explore the Wesleyan campus, where Laura went to college, midway through our trip.

By the end of the first night of Hanukkah, we've lit the candles, sung the Baruch Atah Adonai song, and kissed. By New Year's Eve, we are dating. We move in together officially after two years of living together unofficially.

Our geographic birthplaces are wildly different. We argue often about whether words like "Mary," "marry," and "merry" and "ferry" and "fairy" are said the same way (I think they are) or have different pronunciations (Laura thinks they do). We have to work hard to understand each other's baggage: my struggles to be public about my queer identity given the Hindu conservatism of my family and the Bible Belt conservatism of my West Virginia loved ones; Laura's struggles with anxiety, born out of New York neurosis, then profoundly exacerbated by her experience of being a high school student trapped in a stairwell at Ground Zero on 9/11. But there are also strong through lines in our relationship that bind us through our disconnections: deep passion for the work we do with the young people in our classrooms, strong love for family, an ever-present desire for food and travel adventures.

* * *

"There is no way in hell that you are getting me on that plane."

Laura eyed the propeller plane nervously from the tarmac at Dulles Airport. Flights from Dulles to Charleston, West Virginia, happen on De Havilland Bombardier Dash 8 aircrafts, which can hold about thirty passengers but frequently run empty enough that the flight attendants rearrange passengers to ensure weight is distributed evenly across the length of the plane. These planes are also known for their ability to engage in extremely short takeoffs and landings—a necessary feature when landing on a runway that's basically just a mountain with its pointed peak lopped off.

Our tickets placed us in row 17 of the plane. This had given Laura some small comfort, until she boarded the plane and saw that the row numbering started at 1, progressed sequentially up to row 4, and then suddenly skipped forward to 16, with no rows of seats in between.

For a longtime West Virginian like me, this flight posed no issues. "Puddle jumpers," as we call them, are the primary kind of plane used for getting in and out of Yeager Airport. For my Brooklyn-bred partner, the plane was only the first of many culture shocks to come on our journey back to my childhood home. Taco in a bag, Confederate-flag license plates, Tudor's Biscuit World, the Vandalia Gathering of old-time music and dance, and playing the "hillbilly or lesbian?" guessing game were still on the horizon.

Laura had been my partner for five years before I found the courage to take this trip. I'm ashamed to admit that it took me this long to introduce her to people whom I'd loved my whole life. But growing up, I never knew anyone—neither Indian nor West Virginian—who was openly gay. It wasn't a topic discussed at school, and it wasn't something we talked about at home or in my community. We played Smear the Queer on my street, throwing one another down a grassy hill, without ever questioning the name of the game. I didn't know what the word "gay" really meant, aside from crude insults thrown at less-masculine boys, until I started college. It was only then that I met my first gay West Virginian, in the form of a man from Wheeling who helped me bring a section of the AIDS quilt to campus for viewing during my sophomore year.

"I didn't even know there were gay people in West Virginia," I told him, with a kind of unabashed ignorance that seems to evaporate after college. He calmly assured me that indeed, there were.

Having never heard the topic discussed, when I finally came into my own identity, I found it difficult not to imagine the worst: that it hadn't been discussed because it wasn't condoned.

We landed late in the evening and drove down the winding mountain from the airport, across the river, and into the hills of St. Albans to stay at the home of the parents of my best friend from high school, David. Even as I was going to introduce Laura to my extended family, I was still calculating risk. I decided to stay with the Morrises, whose adult children are both in queer relationships, rather than impose our relationship onto homes where our sleeping in the same bed might have been a source of discomfort.

But over the next two days, my Indian aunties and uncles consistently proved me wrong and showed me how I'd underestimated them. They poured down their love on us in quantities I could never have imagined. They took us out to Joe Fazio's for Italian food. They went to the Liars Contest at the Vandalia Gathering with us and laughed at the tall tales even when they couldn't fully make out the stories for the thickness of the teller's accent. They regaled Laura with horror stories of flying into and out of Charleston's airport, like the time when Yummy uncle's flight was landing and the plane suddenly jerked back into the air, with the pilot announcing, "Oops! I missed."

And above all, they constantly repeated the same refrain, "Ghare aavjo." Come home.

More than anything else, this was the phrase that overwhelmed me. I know my West Virginia family well enough to know that even if they were uncomfortable, they would make it through dinner in a restaurant for the sake of saving face, and for the sake of my parents. But asking us to come home, to drink chai in their living rooms, to stay with them at night—that was different. That wasn't saving face; it was love.

We don't say "I love you" in my community. We cook for you. We host you in our houses. We accept your loved ones as our own. "Ghare aavjo" was the truest expression of unconditional love I could have asked for. It meant that, finally, Laura and I could come home to them together.

* * *

I drag Laura on road trips through the South at least once a year from that point on, causing her to say every time, "Never in my life did I think I would be in . . . Charleston, West Virginia/Birmingham, Alabama/Asheville, North Carolina/the Mississippi Delta." And, without fail, at some point on every single one of our drives through the rural South, "What do the people who live here *do* with their lives?" Which is what happens when you grow up in the center of the known universe. Every other place simply seems boring.

But on our trip to the Mississippi Delta in 2016, Laura's attitude towards my constant banter with strangers began to shift from annoyance to appreciation. She was the first to slow down and chat with two gay men from California in a hipster bar in Jackson. She didn't bat an eye when an artist in Clarksdale saw us admiring his work from the sidewalk, unlocked his shop door, and invited us in to chat for two hours. She even expressed some regard for the slowness of southern life that I have loved my whole life, though sitting still does not come easily to her.

Maybe gnawing on beans isn't so bad after all.

* * *

This is not to say there aren't hard aspects to living in a mixed-mouse household. Laura's mom is Jewish, and her dad is Irish and Italian. A very, very New York mix, but none of those are cultures I grew up in close proximity to. I don't always grasp her dad's dry sense of humor, and we butt heads about politics more often than she'd like us to. I sometimes grow irritated with the emails her mom sends about making sure we know how to open the trunk of a car if we are ever kidnapped and stuffed into the trunk. ("I have a hatchback," I tell Laura after one of these emails. "It's not even *possible* to get stuffed in the trunk.")

She, in turn, has spent far too many hours of her life wandering through West Virginia Walmarts and sitting in Tim Hortons waiting for me to finish visiting with old friends whose views on sexuality I have as yet been unable to discern, and unwilling to test. She has quietly endured family video chats where everyone screams over each other to be heard and the majority of the conversation is in Gujarati, hitting the mute button to ask for translation only when there is a lull.

And our different paces, at times, have been a frustration for each of us.

I grew up in a place where there was a specific order to the evolution of a relationship: first you date, then your parents meet, then you get engaged, then you get married, then you move in together. Maybe, if you're really liberal, you move in when you're engaged. Meanwhile, Laura's view, that of a city kid whose parents divorced when she was two, went something more like: date, move in together, see how it goes. Commitment? Maybe. Marriage? Really, really maybe.

"Why is marriage the ultimate sign of commitment for you?" she has asked me more than once. "People get divorced all the time. It's not like marriage is some guarantee against that."

And while she is right, I can never shake the lingering feeling that I want our relationship on the record. Maybe this encoded desire stems from years of attending southern and Hindu weddings and seeing communities celebrate love together. Or maybe I am just far more square in my thinking than Laura is.

Either way, in these aspects of life, my southern upbringing pushes me to move much faster than Laura is ready to move. Marriage, children—these things were supposed to be done well before I turned forty. But in a relationship, it doesn't work when one person's pace outruns the other's. I've had to slow down, and Laura has had to speed up, and both of us have shifted our expectations, our time frames, our visions for our future together, to accommodate the needs of a partner who grew up on the other side of a cultural dividing line.

Our city mouse/country mouse upbringings can also impact the way we communicate. Laura is blunt and direct; I learned growing up to "might could" my way around issues. Sometimes her bluntness feels sharp to me. And sometimes my indirect communication style can be a source of annoyance for her. "Can you just say what you want directly?" she'll ask me. And though I want to, some combination of southern gentility and Indian repression creates a barrier in my throat, keeping the words from coming out clearly.

Still, Laura sends my family members cards on their birthdays and signs them from me. I send her mom vegetarian recipes and bought her dad a ridiculously expensive bottle of Japanese whiskey for his birthday last year. We both scour the news after an act of gun violence in Boston to ensure that the victim is not a former student, and have held each other far too many times after it has, indeed, been one of the children who we've loved as our own.

Too fast for Laura, I am sure, and too slowly for me, we figured out how to celebrate our relationship in a way that feels right to both of us: formalized enough for me, spontaneous and intimate enough for her. A surprise gathering of just our closest friends and family at our favorite restaurant in Boston, rented for lunch on the Sunday before Christmas in 2019. Guests, who came thinking they were attending a ten-year anniversary celebration, were handed puzzle pieces to assemble into a collage of photographs. Our parents got the last four pieces, which, joined together, formed an image of our wedding certificate and rings. And then, just before the tables filled with small plates of Mediterranean-inspired dishes like pumpkin challah with salty date butter and honey nut spanakopita with celery root tzatziki, we held hands and exchanged Tree of Life rings while our niece read a short poem.

Our communication styles may be different, our paces might not always match, but our understanding of what it means to love, it would seem, is the same.

* * *

The White Mountains are covered in a multicolored carpet of leaves, and we are driving through them together, oohing and aahing at the vibrancy around us. I sit in the driver's seat, and Laura is in the passenger seat beside me. In the back, my older sister, my mom, and my twelve-year-old niece.

This October leaf-peeping trip is a present for my mom's sixty-ninth birthday. And during our weekend of driving and hiking, I have been playing both chauffeur and DJ, mixing a medley of traditional Gujarati garbas, in honor of the Navratri holiday that has just ended, with country music from the seventies and eighties—the first American music my mom fell in love with. Our basement record player spun Kenny Rogers and Dolly Parton on repeat, and those songs, those voices, combined with those of seventies Hindi film music and Gujarati folk garbas, are the soundtrack of my childhood.

In this car, on this drive, I am trying to re-create that soundtrack. When "Islands in the Stream" comes on, my sister, mom, and I all chime in on the chorus, only to be interrupted by Laura.

"Wait, isn't this 'Ghetto Supastar'?" she asks, referring to the 1998 one-hit wonder by the rapper Pras, ODB from the Wu-Tang Clan, and Mýa.

I look at her sideways and laugh. "Laura, 'Islands in the Stream' came out in 1983. Years before 'Ghetto Supastar.' They might have sampled, but this is the original."

This is not the first musical misunderstanding we have had. Once, listening to Florida Georgia Line's song "Simple," I caught Laura mis-singing the lyric about the simplicity of a six-string guitar. Her version of the line went "We're just simple like the 6 train." When I looked at her puzzled, she explained, "You know, the 6 train is simple. It goes straight down the east side from the Bronx to Manhattan." It made sense. For a New Yorker.

Another time, she caught me singing Outkast's "Ms. Jackson" the way only a nerdy Indian spelling bee winner from West Virginia could misunderstand it: "Autonomous Jackson, I am for real." Our roots show most when we are singing, it would seem: mine, of growing up in White, working-class rural America in the late eighties, and Laura's, of growing up in an early nineties Brooklyn where hip-hop was king.

On this drive, Laura suffers through my Ken Burns–style history of country music lecture and continues to sing the lyrics of "Ghetto Supastar" each time the chorus comes up. And I laugh and sing the "Islands in the Stream" version, because this is who we are: Dolly and ODB, country and city. Me singing "from one lover to another," her singing "from one corner to another," both of us at the top of our lungs. The lyrics may be different, but the music underneath remains the same.

Finding the Holy
in an Unholy Coconut

🌱 🌿 🌱

⊙⊙⊙⊙⊙⊙

The idea for plunging a coconut into the ocean came after we'd already decided to drive out to Zuma Beach. In the summer of 2018, Laura and I were on the tail end of a West Coast adventure that had started in Oregon and ended in Los Angeles.

After brunch at utterly hipster, utterly delicious Sqirl, with its crispy rice and lacto-fermented hot sauce, we walked up and down North Virgil in search of a coconut. Sqirl was the anomaly on this edge of Silver Lake, a ten-dollar-avocado-toast outpost marking the beginning of gentrification in an otherwise heavily Latino, heavily working-class enclave. On a block dotted with driving schools, auto repair shops, storefront churches, and a taxi company, we found a carnicería—the only other source of sustenance besides Sqirl in an interminable food desert.

Laura looked at me skeptically. Having been raised in a household that was both Hindu and vegetarian, I get squeamish just walking past the butcher's counter in the grocery store. As age forty-three approaches, I can still visualize every sinew, every tendon, every striation of fat on the skinned deer

I once encountered hanging from a hook in a high school friend's garage.

"Are you sure you want to do this?" she asked.

"I'm sure," I said. "Zuma is where Sam would have wanted his ashes scattered. We don't have his ashes, but we can at least do this for him."

We entered the butcher shop, full of Latino customers and workers, Duranguense blaring on the loudspeaker, and rapidly made our way to the small produce section, me working hard to avoid eye contact with the slabs of meat that seemed to appear in every corner.

I approached a man stocking produce and asked in Spanish, "Perdón, señor. Estoy buscando coco. Lo tienes aquí?"

He led me to another aisle where a small stack of white coconuts rested beside prickly green nopal paddles. I grabbed the one on top of the pile, hurried to the cash register, paid two dollars for my coconut, and headed back out into the blazing California sun.

"That's all we need?" Laura asked.

I looked at the coconut. Sam's mom would be horrified to know its source. A coconut from a butcher shop could only be less holy if it were actually covered in cow's blood. But we were going to Zuma, and I needed a coconut to throw into the ocean. I needed another attempt at finding closure for my cousin's death.

* * *

The last time I threw a coconut into water, I stood on a metal bridge over the Poca River with my mother. It was 2003, and her mother, my grandmother, had just died in India. Seven thousand nine hundred thirty-three miles away in West Virginia, we performed a prayer at the altar in our kitchen, offering the coconut as prasād, a gift for the gods. We adorned it with vermillion powder, then took it to a bridge above the muddy, swirling river a few miles from our house, dropped it into the water, and watched it float away.

It is not customary to throw coconuts into water after someone's death, though Hindus often use coconuts as offerings in rituals, and putting them into the water is considered the only appropriate way to dispose of them afterwards. What comes from the earth gets returned to the earth, the theory goes. But the usual rituals where coconuts come into play are joyful ones: weddings, fertility ceremonies, festivals honoring the relationship between siblings. It is only in my mind that coconuts have come to be associated with death. Only in my mind that throwing them into water is a way to honor the soul of the departed and manifest the grief of those left living.

My grandmother wished that we commemorate her death this way. She wanted us to be able to feel a connection to her passing even from a distance. And for my mother, this coconut was the only ritual that would make her grief tangible—take the pain that existed within her body and put it out into the West Virginian world of our day to day, where no one spoke our language or shared our faith. Where no one knew my grandmother. Where no one driving by on the winding rural road understood why we had parked our car beside the bright-orange river, stained by red West Virginia clay, and stood crying in a rainstorm on a bridge with a coconut in our hands.

* * *

When I first visited Los Angeles in 2013, I met Sam for dinner in Westwood at an Indonesian restaurant a few blocks from his apartment. Laura dropped me there and went to visit her family. Though Sam and I had been very close as children, whiling away months of summer vacation together in our respective hometowns in the Rust Belt, adulthood had taken us to different coasts, and radically different lifestyles: mine as a public school teacher, his as a chemical engineer turned marketing manager. There was much that Sam didn't know about my life, and certainly an equal amount, if not more, that I didn't know about his. I decided to keep my relationship with Laura from him until I had a better sense of who "adult Sam" turned out to be.

Sam was in graduate school at UCLA at the time. Over plates of gado gado and nasi goreng, he eagerly told me about his upcoming business school trip to Japan, where he was most excited about eating a twenty-course, $300 omakase at Jiro's sushi shop. He talked about the research he was doing into buying a new car and about the places he was thinking about working after graduation. His search only included big-name corporations in the Los Angeles area. Why? I had asked him. The weather, he explained. He wanted to live somewhere where the sun shone all the time. This detail didn't strike me as odd when he said it but is one I have returned to often in trying to make sense of Sam's death.

When I asked him for suggestions on places I should explore in his sunny city, his most emphatic recommendation was for Zuma Beach, about an hour north of LA on Highway 1.

Laura and I drove up to Zuma the following day. In February, the Zuma winds carried a chill, leaving the beach completely empty except for the two of us. The glaring reflection of sun on sand made it difficult for me to keep my eyes open. Rough waves, more suited for surfers than swimmers, crashed on the shoreline. A few seals' heads bobbed in the water. That my fairly conventional cousin loved a place so wild surprised me. Cheerful Malibu, I would have understood. Barren, uninhabited Zuma did not match my perception of his style.

I texted him a picture from Zuma, with a short message. "Thanks for the rec. It's truly beautiful here."

He responded. "It's my favorite place out here. I'm so glad you've seen it now."

* * *

As a Hindu living in majority-Christian, majority-Caucasian West Virginia, I learned everything about my faith from my mom, not from any formal religious community. Our community's "temple" popped up in local middle schools, churches, or community centers once a month. Spirituality did not come from a faith community for me; my mother's love served as my embodiment of spirituality. After leaving home, most elements of that spirituality fell away, save my vegetarianism, my need to utter a Hindu prayer every time my plane takes off, and my love of celebrating the Hindu festivals of Navratri and Diwali. For the most part, "high holidays" Hinduism is sufficient. But in moments of inexplicable grief, when my rational mind fails me, I still turn back to my mother's faith, her rituals, as the only paces I can put my mind and body through to assuage my pain.

In the months and years after Sam took his own life in 2015, I tried all the rituals I'd participated in with my mother after her mother's death. I held pujas in my living room, lit incense, listened to Hindu bhajans. I placed a photo of us together as children beside the altar in my pantry. I bought food and delivered it to a local food bank on the anniversary of his death. I donated money in his name to charities whose missions I knew he would have cared about. And while these rituals sometimes allowed a slight release of pressure off my overactive brain, the relief was never more than temporary.

Writing, too, brought brief respite. Though not a form of ritual practiced by my family, telling the story again and again, in overly emotional essays too mawkish for public view, served as a kind of catharsis. I could say things in my writing about Sam's death that I could never say out loud to anyone besides Laura and my sister.

But grief, even when it wasn't pushing hard on the backs of my eyeballs, never went dormant. Our 2018 trip to LA three years after Sam's death was one I found myself dreading, despite the fact that we were going to visit old friends and I was going to meet Laura's family there for the first time.

I couldn't articulate my dread until we arrived, when the sensory stimuli—sunshine, traffic, salt water—triggered an onslaught of memories of Sam. A year before his death, we gathered for a family reunion in Austin over Fourth of July weekend. Sam was present, but also not. When he played with our nieces and nephews, he was as funny and vibrant as ever. My last sweet memory of him involves him wearing a bright-orange T-shirt, doing push-ups on my sister's living room floor with at least two children sitting on his back. But he often went missing, sleeping in for long hours and taking extended breaks away from the family. During these absences, I sometimes exchanged a quizzical glance with my sister or questioned my mom quietly, but they didn't know any more than I did. None of us did until it was too late.

On one of our first traffic-impeded drives through the city, I finally confessed to Laura: I didn't want to be in LA because LA had come to signify the place where life became so unbearable for Sam that he no longer wanted to keep living. I couldn't even pretend to enjoy our time in the city without finding a way to honor his memory first.

This is how we ended up driving across LA, first on city streets, then up the Pacific Coast Highway, on a Friday afternoon with a coconut rolling around in the trunk. Sam, for at least part of his time there, had loved this city. Yet his parents had decided to scatter his ashes in India, at the Triveni Sangam—the place where three rivers meet. This seemed a fitting ritual for them, as Hindus raised in India, but it was a decision that I, the America-born cousin, struggled with. India represented their past and their cultural ties. India didn't necessarily represent Sam's idea of home. For starters, Sam's name was *Sam*. The only cousin of our generation to have an American name. And my cousin was even more Americanized than I, in many ways. He enjoyed eating meat, drinking alcohol, spending time in Vegas, dating freely—all habits ran counter to the conservative culture he was raised within.

Sam's hurried cremation in Los Angeles occurred as soon as the coroner's report was complete; his hasty memorial service was planned by friends and family all operating in a state of shock. It all happened so quickly that I wasn't even able to attend.

Weeks later, I spoke of Sam's smile, his infectious laugh, his enduring love of movies like *My Cousin Vinny* and *Mrs. Doubtfire*, at a Hindu ceremony in a small temple in Maryland, to a room full of mourners who did not make the trip to Los Angeles. I wrote the speech in bits and pieces while on hold with credit card companies and banks to close out Sam's accounts, or in between Google searches about how to inform the Social Security Office of a person's passing or how to close the Facebook accounts of the deceased. In trying to ease the burden the unexpected death of their only child placed on his grieving parents, I left no space for my own grief. Thus, the speech and the ceremony brought no sense of closure.

Zuma. The coconut. This was the goodbye I wanted to give Sam.

* * *

Zuma Beach in August, we learned upon arrival, is a far cry from Zuma Beach in February. Every space in the parking lot housed a car. Blankets and umbrellas dotted the beach, leaving more sand visible than at Malibu, but far less than we'd seen during our previous visit. The wild waves carried surfers to shore and back out again.

In the lead up to this moment, I imagined a solitary scene: me wading out into the blue water alone, casting the coconut out past the breakers, then watching it float out into open water. Instead, I stood with Laura on the shoreline under an unforgiving sun, awkwardly holding a prickly coconut, trying to find an opportune moment to throw the coconut out into the water.

Laura kept lookout, scanning the beach for lifeguards, in pursuit of the perfect moment when the water was free of people, the lifeguards looking in other directions, and the waves receding. Multiple times, I geared up to throw the coconut only to have her say, "Wait! Not yet."

Finally, in a tiny moment of calm, she encouraged me to throw the coconut. I uttered a quiet "This is for you, Sam," then threw the coconut as far as I could manage.

The coconut landed on top of the water with a resounding splat. Instead of sinking or floating out to sea, it bobbled in the waves, then rushed back to shore when the next big wave came in, swirling in the sandy water before landing directly at my feet.

I tried again.

The coconut returned to me.

Laura tried, thinking her arm might be stronger than mine. Still, the coconut returned. There is a reason, it would seem, that Hindus submerge their coconuts in rivers and not oceans. A reason that had escaped me until this moment, when middle school science lessons about buoyancy and salinity came flooding back.

For the next hour, we endeavored to cast the coconut out to sea. When we felt beachgoers' sidelong glances turn into brazen stares, we took the coconut back to our towels, waited for people to get distracted, then headed back to the water. Each time, we waded farther out, our clothes growing heavy with salt water and sand. Each time, no matter how far we threw the coconut, it inevitably landed back on the shore. What began as holy ritual had morphed into a frustrating game of catch that only the ocean seemed to want to play.

The sun dropped low on the horizon. We planned to meet a friend for dinner on the other side of the city at seven o'clock, and it was already close to five. Given LA's notorious crosstown traffic, we had to leave soon if we were going to make it on time.

Laura prodded me gently, as she had done multiple times over the past hour. "I think you may just have to leave it, love. The tide will take it out eventually."

I struggled to abandon the coconut. What if people walking by picked it up, thought it a toy? What if they kicked it? Touching sacred objects, even unholy carnicería coconuts, with the feet is a sign of major disrespect for Hindus. It was bad enough that my coconut came from a butcher shop. Would I leave it now to be desecrated by beachcombers' feet? I threw the coconut out one more time, willing it to take flight, land past the pull of the tide's ebb and flow.

It returned to the beach once more and settled on the sand just above the tide line. I watched from a distance as people walked past it, looking quizzically at this nonnative species inhabiting their beach. A man touched it with his toe. My blood pressure spiked. A child ran up and poked it gingerly with her finger. Another spike.

"We have to go now," I said. "Otherwise I'm never going to be able to leave this coconut. I'll be here 'til midnight throwing it out into the water again and again."

I took a picture of the coconut sitting on the beach, texted it to my sister and cousins. "Tried to put a coconut in the water at Zuma today for Sam. Despite our best efforts, the coconut refused to leave the beach. In a weird way, I think Sam would have loved this."

One cousin responded immediately with a string of heart emojis, followed by this: "I go to the beach every year on his birthday for the same reason. You're right. He definitely would have loved it."

We packed up our towels, trudged through the sand to our car. I took one last look at the coconut on the sand, water droplets clinging to its fibers, both of our forms facing the setting sun and the shining waters of the Pacific, before getting into the car and driving away.

Was it a sign, I wondered, that this coconut refused to float off into the sunset? Lord Varuna, god of the oceans, rejecting my unholy coconut? My half-hearted, haphazard Hinduism failing me in one of the few moments in my life when I really needed it to work? Or was it just science—the coconut too light, the salt water too buoyant, the tide too strong?

This wasn't the way the ritual was supposed to happen. Hell, this wasn't even a real ritual, according to any practicing Hindu. But for a small moment as we pulled out of the parking lot, the pressure on my brain eased a little, and I laughed at the thought of my cousin, who loved this beach so much that his coconut refused to leave its shore.

◎◎◎◎◎◎

Wine-Warmth

🌱🌲🌱

◎◎◎◎◎◎

We are driving in David's indigo Chevy truck, nicknamed Indy, on a warm summer night in 1997. The West Virginia air is heavy with moisture, the sky a velvety black. Indy's high beams light up the unmarked pavement in front of us just enough to ensure that David has time to hit the brakes in the likely case a deer crosses in front of the truck. For city people, this might seem like the opening to a horror movie. For us, it is a regular Saturday night.

The three of us—David, me, and Dave—always sit in the same order in the front of the truck. David drives, because Indy is his and he's the only one of us who knows how to drive stick. Dave gets the passenger seat, because his legs are long. And I am left "riding the hump," as the boys like to tease me, legs crammed into the narrow space between the gearshift and the seat.

On this night, like most every other night we have spent as teenagers in our small town, we have nothing to do. The usual entertainment options—bowling, a movie, getting drunk by the lake at Ridenour Park—do not appeal to us. Instead, we like to drive. We begin at David's house in St. Albans after the sun goes down, then head out Coal River

Road. Ease the truck along the curves of the river. Sometimes we listen to the flow of the water over rocks, the cicadas' constant drone; sometimes we blast the Indigo Girls loud enough to generate a noise complaint. We drive for hours, until we tire. Head home, make a plan to drive again the next weekend.

We have driven like this for four years of high school, since freshman year when David got his license, and truck, at age fifteen. I joke that Dr. Seuss wrote the book *Too Many Daves* about our friendship. David is pure melodrama, full of terrible jokes, and has loving parents who have adopted me as one of their own. Dave exudes calmness and constancy, laughs at all the bad jokes we can muster. They are each other's foils, and I reap the benefit. They make going to a school where Confederate flags threaten and gobs of saliva get hawked onto my head by cowardly racists something I can bear.

This drive will be our last. We leave for college soon. But it does not occur to any of us to say something meaningful, something evocative on this last drive. Instead, we alternately sing and sit in silence.

These friendships will not last. At least, not at this depth of feeling. But this sensation of quiet comfort, of being so known that there is no need to talk, is one I will chase throughout my life.

* * *

The Welsh word for nostalgia is *hiraeth*, though the Welsh argue that nostalgia is too simple a term to describe the complexity of their feelings. Hiraeth is more than missing home, they say. It is missing a sensation and being unable to replicate it.

From Wales, the word and associated feeling traveled to West Virginia in the seventeenth and eighteenth centuries. The Welsh settled in the hills and hollers of West Virginia, and so too did the feeling of hiraeth. Talk to any expat West Virginian, and in the wistful way they describe home, you will hear echoes of hiraeth. A wish to return to a moment, a feeling, that none of us have been able to replicate since.

* * *

For our last meeting of the year, my undergraduate thesis advisor at Carnegie Mellon suggests something fairly shocking to me, an Indian girl raised in a dry household deep in the Bible Belt.

"Bring a bottle of wine with you. We deserve to celebrate."

This thesis has been what many creative nonfiction undergraduate theses tend to be: an excavation of my family's dirty laundry in an attempt to understand it. And Janey has been a willing learner of a different culture, a tireless giver of feedback on hundreds of drafts. Weekly, we hole up in her office for hours talking about the ideas behind the writing. I leave saddled with books each time: more to read, more to learn, more ways to build my writing.

Thirteen years later, the thesis will be placed in an online archive without my knowledge or permission, then discovered by a young cousin in India who is Googling me. My extended family will tear into me for sharing their secrets, and I will no longer be welcome in their homes in India. But in this moment in 2001, sitting in Janey's corner office in Baker Hall with a green glass bottle of Shiraz and clear plastic cups, I feel no anxiety. Only some mixture of relief that I am done and sadness that this relationship, which has grown so deep over the four years of college, will end.

Janey, after all, is the person who came in to work with me on her spring break during my freshman year. Which she did after she gave me a round of feedback in my first writing class, where she said, "You need to make this section into a scene," and my West Virginia–educated response was

"What's a scene?" She is the person who turned me on to Jonathan Kozol in a literary journalism class, and helped me see the connection between my growing love of educating young people and my growing love of the written word. She is the first person who gave me permission to ask questions about gender and Indian culture, and made space for me to speculate about the answers to those questions.

We toast and celebrate the end of our work, and then without warning, Janey looks at the clock, realizes she has another meeting, and kicks me, and the wine bottle, out of her office.

I stagger down the smooth concrete slope of Baker Hall, swig the final dregs from the bottle, and head to my next class. After class, still somewhat tipsy, I take the empty wine bottle, place it in front of Janey's office door with a scribbled note of thanks.

The next time I visit Pittsburgh, nearly a year after moving to Wisconsin, I notice that the empty bottle sits on a shelf in her office, with a wall hanging I brought her from India as the backdrop. I am filled with a warmth not unlike the wine-drunk warmth of that day back in May. I take it as a sign, an artifact. Proof that our relationship didn't just change me.

Twenty-two subsequent years, of back-and-forths about essays, emails about the death of the guinea pig her children named after me, texts about authors we love and don't love, conversations about what it means to forgive ourselves for our transgressions, have only served to bear that out.

Just today, thinking about this story, this feeling I long to recapture, I sent Janey a text. "Do you still have the wine bottle?"

Her response is immediate, fills me with wine-warmth yet again. "Of course I do!"

* * *

There is no word for nostalgia in Gujarati. The closest concept I can find is that of vatan, or homeland. As in: many of the Gujarati immigrants of my parents' generation operated under a narrative that someday, they would return to their vatan. They embraced the desi first law of motion as it were: A desi at rest dreams of her vatan; a desi in motion is always moving towards her vatan. Rarely did they acknowledge that globalization had rendered their vatan unrecognizable. Instead, they filled their children with envy. What did it mean to have such a deep connection to a place? What would it take for us to have a similar connection?

* * *

For thirty years after their immigration from India, my parents reside in a small town in southern West Virginia. But by the mid-nineties my father's initial employer, Union Carbide, sells their local plant off to a French company called Rhône-Poulenc, which then sells the plant off to Bayer Crop Science, which then sells it off to Dow Chemical. With each sale, the plant shrinks. With each sale, more employees receive pink slips.

In 2003, my father receives an ultimatum: Retire or move.

A workaholic aged only fifty-eight, he isn't ready to retire. So they opt to move.

I am twenty-four years old, full of righteous indignation, when my mother announces that they are moving.

We are sitting in our backyard, on the large wooden swing that replaced the smaller swings of my childhood. After dinner each evening during the summer, we retire to the swing, a family custom that has traveled across generations and oceans. The swing is painted maroon, because of paint left over from staining the deck. The metal frame it hangs on is painted a forest green, though chipping corners tell a story of years of spray painting, first a chalky light 1970s green, then bright yellow, then layer upon layer of forest green. This swing set has entertained my childhood friends, hosted lengthy visits from ocean-crossing relatives, even taken part in my sister's wedding rituals. When I close my eyes and envision home, I do not see my childhood bedroom, our living room, our dining room. Instead, it is this swing, this patch of grass with its wide-angle view of my father's garden, that comes to mind first.

"How can you do this?" I ask. "How can you leave this place where we've lived our entire lives? Why can't dad just take a package and retire?"

"Home isn't a place, Neema. It's the people," my mom says. "Your home is where we, your family, are."

This is my mother's definition of home, because for her, it is the truth. India is home because India is where her family lives.

For me, the definition of home is more complicated: a messy combination of people and place. My nuclear family alone doesn't constitute my home. Home is also David and Dave, their parents, our neighbors on Pamela Circle, the aunties and uncles of the local Indian community. People more rooted to place than my wanderlust parents. People who I will lose once my parents leave this place.

The depth of feeling in these relationships will last, but the opportunity to experience it will dwindle over time. My family is split between cities—Austin, where my parents and sister now live; New York, where Laura's family is; and Boston, where we live. West Virginia takes the last number on the list of places to visit. I am lucky if I get there once a year. Feel lucky if I get to experience that wine-warmth of hiraeth, that sensation of being in my vatan, even once a year.

When I purchase my own house in Boston, my first act, before even buying a kitchen table, is to acquire a porch swing. I order it from a carpenter in Tennessee, assemble it, stain it, and install it on my back porch. I inaugurate it during a late summer thunderstorm. Close my eyes, inhale the ozone, pump my legs forward, then back, and try to imagine I am on Pamela Circle once again.

* * *

The Portuguese word for nostalgia is *saudade*, a sentiment best expressed in the melancholic longing of fado songs. In Portugal one summer, I went to a fado concert and picked up the words to a song about the town of Coimbra. The verse I find myself singing most often goes *Coimbra, tem mais encanto na hora de despedida*. Translated, it means "Coimbra, I love you more the closer I get to saying goodbye."

Saudade. A sense of missingness, of lost lovers or homes. The love that remains, even after the objects of that love are gone.

Magic Dust

🌱 🌿 🌱

The magician's house had a stacked stone and white siding facade, with asphalt shingles on the roof, an oversized Chevy truck parked in the driveway, and pots of pink geraniums and red petunias precisely placed out front.

The magician wasn't just a magician. He was a World War II veteran. A skilled welder in the machine shop at Union Carbide. The Mr. Fix-it for everyone who lived on our street, Pamela Circle. Betty's husband, Rick's neighbor, and the proud owner of two bulldogs in a row, first Duke and then Butch. A high school–educated engineering savant with subscriptions to *Smithsonian* and *National Geographic*, devoured as soon as they were delivered. A Freemason, a fact we only learned the day of his burial at the cemetery in Spencer when the Masons came out and conducted a special ceremony on his behalf.

And though he was a White man, born in a rural West Virginia town with an area less than 1.28 miles square, he embraced our Indian immigrant family without blinking when we moved onto his street in 1974. Came to our house for Friday night pizza anytime he was invited. Saved the newspaper for my thrifty father, who refused to pay for his own subscription. Kept our spare key, and never judged me when I went to retrieve it after repeatedly losing my own set. Welded custom magazine racks for dad and sewing machine covers for mom, after hours at the machine shop. Tied chains around the unwieldy bushes in front of our house and yanked them out of the yard with his truck after my mother slipped and shattered all of her metatarsals while trying to tend to them.

He was so much more than a magician, it's true. But for me, he was always the magician first. The gunmetal-green cabinet full of tricks and mysteries in his garage felt reserved only for me.

My first vivid memory is of the magician. Of seeing him walk up the hill of Pamela Circle with Duke. Of me, aged four, being so excited to watch him do a trick that I ran directly off our porch, forgot to descend the concrete steps, and crashed headfirst onto the sidewalk below. The scar on my forehead serves as a perpetual reminder of my first nonfamilial loves: magic and the magician.

In my memories, I see the magician standing before me as he was back in 1983: wisps of white hair falling softly on his forehead, piercing blue eyes, and thick rimless glasses. Dressed, always, in a polo shirt and sky-colored blue jeans worn fuzzy and soft from so many washes. When setting up a trick, he inevitably dug into the shallow pocket of his jeans for Magic Dust, then passed it over his fist before each big reveal.

"Watch me," he'd say every time, playing oblivious to my rapture. I hear his southern accent, the sound I associate most with home, and with childhood, in my ears still.

In his steady, calloused hands, wedding bands disappeared and reappeared, cut pieces of string regenerated like worms, quarters materialized out of thin air, and the card I picked in secret always reappeared as the card he chose out of the deck.

Weekends, he haunted the Milton flea market with his magician friends to learn new tricks and trade out the old, always keeping things fresh for his Pamela Circle audience of one. I remember our shared anticipation around one trick in particular—an elaborate one that involved a story about a wanderer, and included folding playing cards into stained, creased parchment paper—but I cannot reconstruct the trick from beginning to end no matter how slowly I visualize the steps in my mind.

Evenings, I haunted his porch. An odd child from the start, made odder by my brown skin in an Appalachian sea of White, I felt more comfortable with adults than I did kids. I rode bikes, shot hoops, and played in the creek during the day, and I showed up for Spotlight when the streetlights came on because I knew those were the things kids were supposed to do, but those in-between hours, when the sun dropped low in the sky, were not spent with my peers. Instead, I spent them with the magician on his porch, listening as he discussed gardens and home repairs, trucks and chemical plant politics with his friend Ronnie.

For a short time in elementary school, I tried to emulate the magician in my own way. Convinced my mom to sew me a cape and a top hat, whittled a crooked stick pulled from the oak tree in the backyard and painted it black and white to look like a wand. In photographs, I look like a small, brown chimney sweep, or an Indian Abraham Lincoln, or potentially, due to a serious case of buck teeth, a culturally confused vampire. I bought magic tricks at Spencer Gifts: cheap plastic boxes that hid dollar bills, hollow coins, trick cards. I put on shows for my friends at sleepovers, but could never capture the magician's realness, his sleight of hand, the slow, hypnotic banter that was his and his alone. I never told the magician about these endeavors, and I set them aside before I reached middle school.

I don't remember when the magician's tricks stopped for me. Maybe when I reached high school and grew too busy to wander down the street to the magician's garage. Certainly when I went away to college and only saw him briefly on my visits home. All I know is that there came a point when I lost sight of the magic. Worse, when I lost sight of the magician.

And then one day during my junior year of college, Butch got loose during the magician's visit to his friend Kenny Bell's auto shop in Nitro. Ran across the street and onto the railroad tracks. The same tracks that carried chemicals to and from the plant where the magician worked between high school graduation and retirement, with only a brief battlefield hiatus. And the magician, who loved his dogs like others love their children, whom I loved the way American children loved their grandparents, ran onto the tracks to save Butch.

Maybe he misjudged the distance between the oncoming train and himself. Maybe Butch couldn't hear him calling over the roar of the train. But the magician died that day, while Butch survived. Leaving the rest of us with just artifacts of his existence: welded boxes, blocks of beeswax, old copies of his magazines.

Twenty years later, I still stand at the foot of the driveway to the magician's stone house on Pamela Circle on visits home. Wait for him to open the garage door, rummage through the cabinet, and then emerge with a new trick up his sleeve and Magic Dust in his pocket.

A Hindu Hillbilly Elegy

🌱 🌱 🌱

⊙⊙⊙⊙⊙⊙

1.

When I hear the first strains of "Om Jai Jagdish Hare," I am instantly five years old again and racing around the exterior of the South Charleston Junior Women's Club with my friends. We throw salted peanuts into cups of Coke, and scream with joy at the ensuing eruptions of brown foam, only stopping when ordered into the building by our parents for the final stage of the puja—the aarti, the moment when light is offered to the deities.

Out of breath and sticky handed, we push our way to the front of the room, where photos and idols cluster on a small table weighed down by offerings of fruit and sweets. Aunties in silken saris hold a flat silver thali decorated with designs made in rice and vermillion powder, upon which small cotton balls dipped in ghee have been lit. One by one, we approach them and take hold of one side of the thali, keeping our eyes on the flames and the idols as we move the thali through the air. First left, then right, then counterclockwise. As each of us finishes, we pass one hand over the flame, then over our heads, a motion ingrained in our muscle memory.

Around us, elders clap their hands and sing the aarti, full throated.

We are a motley crew, this band of Hindus, gathering once a month to pray in southern West Virginia in the mid-1980s. Our families immigrated to the United States from all over India, sometimes by way of Kenya, Tanzania, or Uganda. Work as engineers or physicians has brought us to this tiny state, whose "W" our parents confuse with "V" because we don't have a "W" sound in our home languages. In their mouths, "West Virginia" often becomes "Vest Virginia."

We live in a valley nestled by a river whose name we also struggle to pronounce—Kanawha (another "W" to deal with)—in topography wholly unfamiliar to us. The leaves changing color each fall and then drifting to the ground in crunchy piles is a phenomenon that will perpetually fill us with amazement.

Our immigration to Almost Heaven, West Virginia, began in the late 1960s. By 1990, Asians made up 0.4 percent of the state's 1.7-million-person population. Cut that number in half, eliminating the Filipino, Chinese, and Korean communities, and you have the number of South Asians in the state. Cut that number down to Indians of the Hindu faith, and you have less than 2,000 people statewide. A single Christian megachurch in my hometown had as many members in its congregation as our entire faith did in the whole state.

Hinduism, in its nonpolemicized form, is a loose amalgam of texts, mythologies, philosophies, and rituals. It isn't held together by a pope or a network of clergy. Our priests act as conductors of ritual, not spiritual advisors. In truth, our religion is largely self-directed and individualized. Which is fine when you live in a country where many of the other one billion inhabitants also practice their faith that way. Where there is a temple on every corner and your religion's holy days are state-sanctioned holidays.

Adherence to the faith proved more difficult for me, often the only Hindu in a crowd of Christian classmates. I know this is not just a Neema problem. Nearly every week, I see an article proclaiming the erosion of faith in America. But that erosion, in my case, was both enacted upon me and by me.

2.

"I heard that people like you worship cows."

I was in elementary school the first time someone hurled this phrase at me, much the same way a bloody cow's head had been hurled at the door of our makeshift temple in the basement of a house once in the late seventies.

How does a child explain faith to another child? "We don't worship cows. We just think they are sacred." Worship. Sacred. To a Christian kid in West Virginia with limited vocabulary, what was the difference? My polytheistic faith was incomprehensible.

The blue gods, the ones with elephant heads, the ones whose stories my mother recounted and I hungrily devoured, were mocked by my classmates in the world outside our home.

"Why don't you eat meat?" they would ask, eyeing my fluo-rescent-yellow lemon rice, stained by turmeric and packed in a biohazard Ziploc bag my thrifty father had taken from the chemical plant. The orange skull and crossbones on the front did nothing to ease my outsider status.

"Hindus don't believe in violence. Killing animals is a form of violence, so we don't eat meat." I gave them the same answers my parents had given me when I asked at our dinner table. But the answers I accepted unquestioningly didn't suffice.

"What if plants have feelings? What if that carrot is actually screaming when you cut into it? Aren't you committing violence then?"

Again, I failed to know how to explain. So much of culture and faith had been automated for me, much as they had been for my Christian peers, that I couldn't provide reasoned responses to their questions. It never occurred to me to turn the microscope on them, on their faith, on their culture. Such is the curse of being the minority during childhood, I suppose. It never quite feels safe to challenge dominance in that way.

Instead, their shaming questions pricked tiny holes in my nascent faith, tapping any reserves built up at home and at puja.

3.

My bedtime routine as a child was the same every night. My mom came into my room and patted my back as she sang Gujarati and Sanskrit bhajans to me. I fell asleep each night to the sounds of "Raghupati Raghav" and "Vakratunda Mahakaya," learning the words long before I learned the meanings.

When I sought to understand, instead of just parrot, and deliberately asked my mom to translate word for word, pushing her knowledge of Sanskrit vocabulary beyond its limits, I sometimes found the songs didn't resonate with me. Singing about Ganpati's curved trunk, round body, and brilliance of a hundred suns didn't fill me with a sense of spirituality. It was my mom's voice that convinced me all was right in the world, not the words she was singing. I remember wanting desperately to emulate her piety, but failing to understand the source of her devotion. I sang the songs, replicated the rituals, hoping to capture the same holiness I saw on her face when she stood at the altar in our kitchen. Still, no matter how hard I stared at my reflection in the tiny silver idols, I never saw that same look mirrored on my face.

But I'd be lying if I told you that I don't sing those bhajans to myself at night when I have trouble sleeping. Or that I don't say a quick "Bhagvan badha nu bhalu karjo/Bhagvan badha nu rakshan karjo" every time I board a plane, asking God to forgive my mistakes and keep me safe. Or that I didn't listen to "Raghupati Raghav," Gandhi's favorite hymn, on repeat six years ago when my cousin committed suicide at the age of thirty, and I inexplicably set up the idols on my altar in front of his picture, lit incense, and sang along.

4.

A sampling of conversion attempts by Christians, in chronological order:

1986: A neighbor invites me to attend Sunday school with her. I pressure my mom into letting me go, and after a few sessions, find myself up at the altar being saved. My mom never lets me go back to Sunday school again.

1992: My middle school basketball coach forces our team to say the Lord's Prayer before every game. Participation is not optional. I can still recite it verbatim today. "Our father, who art in Heaven, hallowed be thy name."

1994: A Mormon high school classmate sends blond-haired, black-suited missionaries to my house. My parents keep the Book of Mormon that is proffered, unsure of how to turn it down, but politely send the missionaries on their way.

1996: A friend invites me to a Super Bowl party at her church. All goes well until halftime, when the pastor turns off the television and asks for people to bow their heads, then encourages people in the room who are ready to accept Jesus into their hearts to raise their hands. I am the only person in the room who is not already a member of the church. I squeeze my eyes shut tight, keep my head bowed, and count the minutes until halftime is over and the game begins again.

And then there is the constant question asked every time our brown-skinned family attends a gathering of White West Virginians.

"Have you been saved?"

"Have you been saved?

"Have you been saved?"

The litany is exhausting. The holes in the fabric of my faith grow larger. I don't seek to patch them up with Christianity. I simply wish I did not have to explain or justify my inherited, out-of-place identity.

5.

My favorite family photo depicts three Indian couples on an autumn road trip. The men, complete with shocks of thick, black hair and patterned bell-bottom pants, the women, with luxurious braids and chandlos painted on their foreheads, stand in front of a log grist mill, the red and orange leaves of West Virginia fall scattered around them. Their children, ranging in age from infancy to ten years old, squirm on laps and scramble towards the edges of the frame.

Each fall, my parents organized a trip to a state park in West Virginia for us and the other West Virginia Gujaratis who became our inherited family. At Pipestem or Hawks Nest or Blackwater Falls, we hiked through deciduous forest, waded in creek beds, rode horses, and sang Bollywood songs and Hindu bhajans by the light of a campfire. We ate khichadi for dinner and Teays Valley biscuits for breakfast.

Through these trips, I grew to love the wild and wonderful aspects of West Virginia, even as I struggled with the religious and racial elements. Its natural beauty settled into my sensory memory right next to the Hindu puja. West Virginia is the only home I know, though it is not a home that always loves me back.

The same holds true for many of my peers from the Hindu hillbilly crew, the rowdy children who played until it was time to go in for puja. While the tug-of-war between the culture of their homeland and the culture of their new home certainly existed for my parents and their friends, the impact on their identities seemed far less extensive than it was for the Indian American young people of my generation. By the time our parents moved to America, their identity formation was largely complete. Their work, in some senses, was about re-creating the sensory experiences and rituals of their past. But they always had their past as a point of reference.

For young people in our community, the challenge was different. As adolescents, deep in the throes of identity formation, holding to our parents' religious faith was much harder. We didn't have the same emotional attachment to the rituals, the sensory memory of what the holidays actually felt like, or what it felt like to share those holidays with family. We had modified rituals, simulations of holidays, held in incongruous spaces with fluorescent lighting and shiny linoleum flooring. My mom waxes nostalgic about doing Navratri garba for all nine nights growing up in India. I only know the experience of two weekend garbas held in the same middle school gymnasium where I took phys ed from Monday through Friday.

If anything, the closest approximation to faith for me might be the omnipresent pull to go home to the Mountain State. The way the colors of a West Virginia fall still render me breathless. How the lyrics of John Denver's "Country Roads" evoke an enormous lump in my throat. It is the "hillbilly" part of my upbringing that has stayed with me, even as so many of the Hindu elements slowly fall away.

6.

One year, when my sister and I both inhabited the teen sector of the age spectrum, my parents decided it wasn't enough for us just to visit family on our sporadic trips to India. We needed to see the country more broadly. They took us on a trip to South India. A trip on which I often found my angsty teen-self moaning, "Not *another* temple" or "Not *another* palace."

My aversion stemmed partially from being a teenager, and so opposed to any idea my parents had. But I also felt disturbed by the rules that many temples posted out front: Menstruating women were not allowed to enter. Women whose clothing showed their shoulders or legs were not allowed to enter. Men wearing pants and not lungis—a kind of male sarong—were not allowed to enter.

I wore gaudy Jams shorts and a white T-shirt. My sister had on a sleeveless, shapeless dress. My father wore his usual pants and collared shirt. Vendors outside the temple hawked rented lungis and scarves, urging my father to take them.

He barked at them angrily, muttering, "I'm not giving you money for that dirty fabric."

Effectively, at each of these temples, the only person allowed to enter was my mom, dressed in the traditional sari. The rest of us had to wait for her outside.

Waiting outside only served to further my discomfort. Hungry children in tattered clothing looked at us with pleading eyes, bringing their hands to their cracked lips in an eating gesture. Flies buzzed around the head of a man suffering from elephantiasis, a condition caused by parasitic worms that resulted in his leg swelling to massive proportions—like those of an elephant—rendering him immobile. The contrast between the smooth, indulgent marble and gold of the temple and the ashy, wrinkled texture of the skin stretching over the pauper's swollen leg was too much for me to handle. This wasn't the warm and communal Hinduism of the Junior Women's Club that I knew and loved. This was organized, institutionalized religion, with all its classed and gendered hypocrisies. And suddenly I wasn't sure I wanted to be Hindu anymore.

7.

I thought I knew the rituals of Hindu weddings well. The circles my sister and her future husband Kumar would take around the fire. The seven steps they would take, making a vow with each step. I knew that our brothers would throw rice into the fire to symbolize their support of my sister as she entered married life. But typing up English translations of the various phases of the ceremony for my sister's wedding, I reached a stage that confounded: the point in the ceremony where married women were supposed to approach my sister and whisper this phrase—*akhand saubhagyavati*—into her ear.

"Mom, how would you translate *akhand saubhagyavati*?" I asked.

My mom answered without hesitation. "It means 'May you die before your husband.'"

"I'm sorry. What?"

"It comes from the time when women were still forced to commit sati if their husbands died before they did. So, women would wish each other an early death in order to avoid the prospect of being burned on the funeral pyre."

Her tone was calm, clear, and matter-of-fact. Meanwhile, my twenty-two-year-old brain filled with righteous feminist rage. My sister, in the final months of her final year of residency, did not have time to engage in this level of detail when it came to her wedding. It was up to me to delete the description from the program.

"We're not doing that," I proclaimed, pounding delete on the keyboard for emphasis.

My mom was adamant that the ritual of women blessing the bride remain part of the ceremony. So we found a compromise: In accordance with my mom's wishes, on my sister's wedding day, nine women from our community approached my sister and whispered in her ear. In accordance with mine, instead of saying the akhand saubhagyavati of previous generations, they whispered their own personal wishes for a happy and successful marriage. I watched proudly from the first row, feeling, for once, like I had managed to merge the traditions of my heritage with the ethos of my American upbringing.

8.

In my adult life, ritual has fully supplanted faith when it comes to the question of religion. My partner, Laura, is the product of a Catholic father and a Jewish mother. In October, we go to Navratri garbas held in middle schools in the northern suburbs of Boston. In November, we celebrate Diwali by cooking a big dinner and setting off illegal fireworks. We have a menorah and a Christmas tree in our living room in December, and the tree is decorated with a hodgepodge of ornaments representing a set of identities that could only happen in our home: a menorah and an Om, Brooklyn and West Virginia, Ruth Bader Ginsburg, Frederick Douglass, pickles, pizza, and rainbows. A tiny altar sits in our pantry, upon which reside Hindu idols, along with a glass Jesus that a student gave me as a gift. Guilt prevents me from discarding it. Sometimes Laura comes home to the pervasive smell of incense. Sometimes I fry up a batch of latkes to celebrate Hanukkah. But rarely, usually only in case of a marriage, a funeral, or a high holiday, do either of us cross the threshold of temples, synagogues, or churches.

And when it came to our own marriage, the decision to have a very secular, very simple wedding was easy for us to make but difficult for my family to handle. The night before the ceremony, my sister said to me, "It's really hard for me that there will not be any vidhi at your wedding." But neither Laura nor I could imagine a ceremony where we turned to deeply religious, deeply gendered rituals to commemorate our queer, secular relationship.

Still, some elements of my childhood faith are hard to let go of. Last summer, Laura and I made one of our favorite drives—through the Fort Pitt Tunnel, a dimly lit cavern of concrete and tile that spits drivers out onto a bridge with a stunning view of the miniscule but well-placed Pittsburgh skyline. She loves the drive because it reminds her of *The Perks of Being a Wallflower* and the feeling of being "infinite." I love the drive because it reminds me of childhood trips to Pittsburgh for Indian groceries, a visit to the Hindu temple, and a momentary reminder that there are indeed places in America where Indians make up more than 0.2 percent of the population.

"You know where Hindus on the East Coast ask for their ashes to be scattered?" I asked.

"Pittsburgh, I'm guessing?"

"Yeah, but do you know why?"

She didn't. Why would she?

Pittsburgh is the Triveni Sangam of the East Coast. The

place where three rivers meet. In India, the most holy place for ashes to be scattered is at the confluence of the Yamuna, the Ganga, and the Sarasvati rivers. Pittsburgh is the American equivalent: the site where the Monongahela and the Allegheny converge to form the Ohio.

My mom wishes for her ashes to be scattered in Sedona, Arizona, but I know that after the West Virginia University School of Medicine is done with my father's donation of his body to science, his ashes will be scattered at this confluence. So too will those of my American citizen aunts and uncles. This Triveni Sangam is my family's burial ground.

The Judeo-Christian concept of burial is something I can't get my head around—a slow, suffocating decomposition at the hands of soil and worms. I briefly considered the Zoroastrian method, having my body placed on top of a mountain for birds to take heavenwards in their beaks, but this seems both bloody and impractical. In the end, this Hindu ritual is what I want: cremation. Ashes, the throwing of a blessed coconut into the water, the utterance of hymns I've been singing since childhood. A way to return to the mix of Hinduism and Appalachian heritage that have defined me from the beginning.

"Scatter my ashes in Pittsburgh," I told Laura.

From Pittsburgh, those ashes will float downstream. Winding west, then south, to Wheeling, Moundsville, Parkersburg, Ravenswood, and eventually to Point Pleasant, where they will mingle with the waters of the Kanawha, slowly carrying me homewards.

Neighbors

An empty 750-milliliter bottle of Tito's Handmade Vodka sits on its side on the front porch of my house, a green and white Victorian triple-decker in the Boston neighborhood of Jamaica Plain. I am unsurprised.

An hour earlier, my friend Craig had texted me a warning: "Just saw your neighbor staggering down the street with two bottles of vodka in his hands. Wanted to give you a heads up."

I gingerly place the vodka bottle in the recycling bin, sending it to be melted down with the many other nips and full-sized bottles discovered in our yard, hallway, and mailbox over the last two years. Once upstairs, I make a call to the absentee landlord for Unit 2.

"Hi, it's Neema. I came home today to an empty bottle of vodka on the porch. This situation is getting out of hand. Please call me back when you can."

These calls have become more frequent, the tone of my voice more stressed each time, in the eighteen months since Laura first opened the front door of our building on a frigid winter day in early 2017 only to have our second-floor neighbor Johnny collapse on the floor in front of her, his pants down to his knees. She cried out to me, thinking he was dying, then fled to our third-floor apartment in fear. I called 911 and attempted to describe his symptoms—inability to stand up, shortness of breath, incoherent mumbling—only to have Johnny's partner rush out of their apartment to disclose that he wasn't dying, just terribly drunk. That Johnny had struggled with alcoholism for years, and that his addiction had grown so large it could no longer be shoved into the closet.

In the eight years leading up to this moment, Johnny existed in my mind as a lovely, if unusual, neighbor: cologne-laden and exuberant, always greeting us with warm but anachronistic phrases like "Hey, Doll," and gushing at how beautiful we looked when we ran into him on our way out of the house on special occasions. Every fall, he decorated our stoop with mums and pumpkins; every winter he gifted us an enormous red poinsettia and pine bough wreath.

One October, when the mayor declared a state of emergency in Boston because of an impending hurricane, he left us a Styrofoam cooler of hurricane preparedness items: mango and passionfruit vodka, paper towels, candles, and a flashlight. When Laura fell off our porch swing and broke her shoulder, Johnny came running up the stairs, his distended belly jutting out from his undershirt, and refused to leave her side until the paramedics took her out on a gurney.

But there were clues, also, that all was not well under Johnny's cheerful veneer. At night, our floor vibrated from the hum of a machine that was supposed to help Johnny breathe. When sorting the mail, we noticed that the majority of envelopes in Johnny's name came from insurance companies, hospitals, or Social Security. And Johnny's partner, Warren, moved in and back out again multiple times during the course of their relationship, though I never knew Johnny well enough in the early years to understand why.

In truth, there was much I didn't know about Johnny. I knew that he had been the manager at high-end hotels in Boston and San Francisco before getting ill, but it was only in his obituary that I learned he once worked as a costumed character on Fisherman's Wharf and that he was the lightman at some of San Francisco's most popular gay nightclubs in the eighties. Upstairs in our apartment, I was reading Alexander Chee's *How to Write an Autobiographical Novel* to understand more about the history of ACT UP and the fight for gay rights. It never occurred to me that someone in my own house might have borne witness to that history.

The day after our discovery of Johnny's battle with alcoholism, he left a huge bouquet of flowers and an apology note in front of our apartment door. "I am so embarrassed," he wrote in a virtually illegible scrawl. "I will never do it again."

As I am the child of teetotalers who immigrated from one of only four dry states in India, and only an occasional drinker myself, an almost encoded surge of judgment surfaced within me. I didn't even want to bring the flowers into the house. I referred to them as guilt flowers, the kind an abuser would give to the abused after a violent episode, and threw them in the compost as soon as they showed the slightest signs of fading. It wasn't just snobbery fueling my rage, though. I sensed the first drunken episode would not be the last.

Indeed, it wasn't.

A few weeks later, Laura and I heard loud clanking and banging on our back landing late at night. Frightened, we huddled under the covers until the sounds stopped. The next day, Warren called to tell me that we needed to lock up our alcohol, as Johnny had been coming upstairs to steal from our liquor cabinet. He had asked the liquor store owners in close proximity to refuse to sell to Johnny. In turn, Johnny resorted to stealing. When we checked the cabinet on the back landing, entire bottles had disappeared, while others had been largely drained of their contents.

* * *

Although I haven't lived on Pamela Circle for nearly twenty-two years, I can still create a mental map and recite the names and house numbers of every family that lived on my street growing up.

I recall the names of neighborhood dogs long dead—Zeke and Duke and Bonnie and Butch. I can give you a memory I made in virtually every house on the street and with virtually every person who lived there.

I grew up in a place where the word "neighbor" did not just indicate geographic proximity; it possessed the kind of emotion we more often attribute to relationships like "mother" or "lover." My favorite aunt in India, who has lived in the same apartment complex in Ahmedabad for the last forty years, often likes to say that the relationship between those who live together is even stronger than the bond between family members. That when you go through your daily paces together, you understand each other in a way that family cannot.

This was particularly true for my nuclear family. Our West Virginian neighbors were eight thousand miles more proximate than the majority of our blood relations. My parents shared childcare responsibilities, garden produce, household repairs, and responsibility for the ill and the elderly, not with their siblings, but with their neighbors. In a town where the ambulance was sometimes a half-hour drive away, my dad played first responder to heart attacks and hemorrhages, while my mom cooked comfort meals and sat with those in mourning.

More often than not, I was the messenger for my parents' expressions of neighborliness. I delivered the bulging plastic bags of garden tomatoes, peppers, corn, and eggplant, the paper plates of Christmas cookies, the recipes and obituaries clipped from the *Charleston Gazette*. And by observing my parents, I learned early what it meant to be the kind of neighbor who sits on the porch and listens to stories without feeling the need to rush home, who lends a hand to make light work. Being a good neighbor was perhaps among the most prized of qualities in my house growing up, right up there with being a strong student and being a reliable employee.

I would not be who I am today without my neighbors. Without Mr. Withrow, who shot hoops with me on Saturday mornings and taught me how to drive when my father found he didn't have the patience for the job. Without Mr. Starcher, who built me my first clubhouse, taught me magic tricks, and showed me that being educated wasn't about how many degrees you held, it was about the way you read, the way you questioned, the way you made yourself a learner of the world around you. Without Mr. and Mrs. Carney, who stocked their fridge and pantry with snacks I liked and made their home my second one.

Be present. Listen well. Share your bounties. Look for ways to help. Those were the unspoken lessons I learned from my neighbors on Pamela Circle. And they are the ones I try to live out in my work and in my personal relationships.

* * *

A short while after my discovery of the vodka bottle on this warm May evening, Laura calls me. She is driving around the neighborhood looking for a parking spot and has caught sight of our neighbor.

"Johnny has been sitting in his car without moving for ten minutes," she tells me. "He doesn't seem to be able to get the door shut. He doesn't look good."

I look out the kitchen window and see Johnny get out of the car, and partially close the door. He opens the door again, then falls into the driver's seat. He struggles to find the coordination and strength needed to actually shut the door, his hand unable to grasp the door handle to pull it shut. From my perch three stories up, it almost feels like I'm watching a loop GIF in which the character keeps reaching for the handle, missing, and then trying again.

"I think you should call 911," Laura tells me, her voice full of concern.

I don't want to call the police, however. I worry about how Johnny may respond to them. Worry that if he acts aggressively, they may hurt him. I equivocate, try to put the responsibility for calling the police on Laura, if that's what she wants to do.

"Love, he could have killed someone the last time he got in a car," she reminds me. "You need to call 911."

Just a week earlier, Johnny got drunk before 7 a.m. and managed to flip his car less than a thousand feet from our house. I still cannot grasp the sheer physics of this, neither the speed required nor the level of erratic steering necessary to put an SUV on its head within such a short distance from its parking spot. Our street is heavy with foot traffic—students walking to four elementary and middle schools within short distance, commuters heading to the train station at the bottom of the hill. It is difficult to imagine how he could have totaled his car without killing or maiming anyone. Yet the police let Johnny go with a warning, and now here he is, about to drive drunk again, this time when all of those same students and commuters travel homewards.

Johnny's prior drunken episodes have left me uncertain of how to approach him. After eight years of neighborly pleasantries, his battle with alcohol, and the way it impacts those who live both above and below him, has become the defining feature of our relationship. Warren has broken up with him and struggles to balance his sense of responsibility to

someone so clearly ill with his own need for a healthy relationship. Johnny is alone in his apartment with his alcohol.
Laura and I, and my first-floor neighbor, are alone in our
building with Johnny. There is no Warren to serve as a buffer
any longer.

Sometimes Johnny turns aggressive, sneering and cursing
from his vantage point on the stairwell where he has stum-
bled and fallen, while we are trying to help him up. Sometimes he acts incoherent and childlike, and repeats the same
ideas over and over, as was the case when he locked himself
out of his apartment on a winter day and then pounded on
our doorways unceasingly, begging us to let him in, before
ultimately lying down on the first floor in the foyer and rolling around for twenty minutes.

Each time I find Johnny drunk, I channel my inner teacher,
maintain my composure, speak with him rationally, try to
de-escalate the situation. Inside, I am shaking, but I do not let
him see. I try to think about what a good neighbor should do,
what my Pamela Circle neighbors would have done in a similar situation, but come up short. The difference, on Pamela
Circle, was that we did not neighbor alone. We worked together, helped each other, grieved together. Alone, I am not
enough. And this is not a state of being that I am accustomed
to.

Johnny's family lives in California. His parents are elderly;
his sister's husband suffers from Parkinson's. None of them
are able to give Johnny the care he needs. He is alone, with
the exception of Warren and us, his neighbors. I call the landlord after each incident. He has known Johnny for years, and
I beg him to get involved, but he lives in Florida and isn't able
to grasp the severity of the situation. I call Warren, say that
I know it is awkward because they are broken up, but that I
don't know who else to call. We commiserate about Johnny's

struggles, but Warren feels conflicted about how to help without getting re-enmeshed in an unhealthy relationship.

When I call the local police station seeking help on the evening when Johnny is rolling around in the foyer, they say there is nothing they can do about a person who is drunk within their own house, and suggest that next time, I keep him locked out of the building completely so that he can be arrested for public drunkenness. I am shocked by their callousness, and by the failure of our society to have any other kind of safety net for people struggling with addiction. Am I the only safety net? How can this possibly be the case?

Based on previous experience, I am unconvinced that I can keep him from getting in his car on this day in May. At Laura's insistence, and remembering the police officer's advice about seeking support when Johnny is outside the house, I call 911 for the fifth and final time.

"My downstairs neighbor has consumed at least one, and most likely two, full-size bottles of vodka within the last three hours," I tell the dispatcher. "He is at his car now, trying to get the door to close so that he can drive. He has already wrecked one car while drunk, and I am frightened that he may hurt himself or someone else."

I wait at the window. Watch as the police pull up to the intersection of Boylston and St. Peter and approach Johnny. They talk to him gently for over thirty minutes, distracting him away from his car every time he attempts to return to the driver's seat. Eventually, an ambulance comes, and Johnny is strapped on to the stretcher, an image I have become far too accustomed to seeing. One of the officers on the scene calls me and tells me they have gotten Johnny a bed at a residential rehab program and he will be away for three weeks.

I have called the police on my neighbor and gotten him institutionalized. I do not know how to feel about this fact.

* * *

I learned to love my Pamela Circle neighbors deeply, more, perhaps, than I loved members of my own family. Each loss on our street has been a source of profound and sustained grief. Losses we still talk about with sorrow today. Yet those relationships had depth long before death, held a kind of emotional equality I never found with my downstairs neighbor, even though he, too, would leave plastic bags bulging with produce hanging on my doorknob after his trips to Haymarket.

Indeed, on Boylston Street in Boston, where I have lived for the last eleven years, I am barely able to name the neighbors who live in the four houses directly adjacent to mine. I only know the house next door as the "clown house" because one of the women who lives there occasionally comes out dressed as a clown. I know they vote Republican because of their lawn signs. That they used to drive a car service until the old man totaled his car turning the corner. I heard the crunch of metal and the shouts of the people who witnessed the crash, watched his car get towed home, and still did not find a way to engage with him. I have no memories with these neighbors, only memories of them.

I tried to figure out how to support Johnny in the best ways I knew. I Googled addiction support resources. I talked to a colleague whose son struggled with addiction. Again and again, I got the same answer: you can't help someone who isn't ready to get help themselves. And while I understood this, it also filled me with despair.

Being neighborly on Pamela Circle meant keeping doors unlocked and fridges stocked. I ate pickle sandwiches and chocolate pudding at Mrs. Carney's house nearly every day after school because she bought the groceries my parents never would. It meant that no one complained when I started pounding my basketball on the pavement at 8 a.m.; instead they came out to play with me. The saying "good fences make good neighbors" has never really made sense to me because on Pamela Circle, the lines separating neighbor from friend, and friend from family, completely faded away.

But here in Boston, in the context of addiction, everything I was reading and being told urged me to do the opposite: to maintain a firm boundary. To seek punitive measures because no corrective ones existed. Was I just supposed to watch Johnny descend into a death spiral, killing himself just a little bit more with each bottle of liquor he consumed?

Later that winter, Laura and I awoke at 3 a.m. to the sound of a horrible crash on the second floor. An ambulance was at the house within minutes. We learned the next day from the landlord that Johnny had suffered an alcohol-induced seizure and almost choked on his own tongue. He was hospitalized for a few days, enough time to enter withdrawal, then discharged. Within days of him being home, I saw empty nips thrown beneath the bushes in our yard.

As these incidents increased in frequency, I dreaded going home, dreaded seeing my neighbors. My feelings about Boylston Street stood in direct contrast to my feelings about Pamela Circle. Pamela Circle was home, the place where I knew how to be my best self. At Boylston Street, I only felt like I was failing. The skill set my West Virginia neighbors equipped me with, perfect for virtually every social situation, did me no good when it came to Johnny.

* * *

The doorbell rings at 5 a.m. It is insistent, alternating between the bell for our unit and the bell for the first floor. I know without looking that it is Johnny. That he has signed himself out of the rehab facility within less than twelve hours of being admitted and is back to drink some more. The police have taken his keys, so he has no way in to the apartment. He needs us to let him in, but I am full of shame for having called the police on him and anger at him for not accepting the help he needs.

I feel my jaw lock into its stubborn position. Refuse to answer the door. That he continues to ring the bell incessantly indicates that my first-floor neighbor feels the same way. She, too, is exhausted by this cycle of drunkenness, police and ambulance involvement, apologies, and further drunkenness. It is warm outside, and I will leave for school within an hour. I want to punish him. I want to make him wait.

The bell rings and rings and rings for the next hour. I twist in the sheets and seethe. At Johnny. At myself. I am theoretically full of empathy for people who struggle with addiction. I teach my students about the difference between seeing addiction as a failing or a crime and seeing it as an illness. We learn about decriminalization, safe injection sites, about how any citizen can carry Narcan as an antidote to overdose, all of the ways in which our society could do better by those struggling with addiction. And yet with Johnny, my empathy reserves are depleted. Worn down by too many instances of seeing his body writhing on the floor, too many 911 calls, too many bouquets of guilt-scented flowers and apology-filled cards, only to be followed by yet another instance of self-destructive drunkenness. I am both filled with cruelty and ashamed by my own cruelty.

I unlock the door at 6:20 when I leave the house, brush past him without speaking. We will not see each other again before he moves out, evicted by the landlord who has tired of my calls.

* * *

When I run my mental checklist of actions I could have taken on Johnny's behalf, there is only one that remains unticked. What if I erased the line between neighbor and friend, and confronted him? I imagine going downstairs one evening, knocking on the French doors to his apartment, addressing him directly. "You're sick, Johnny," I tell him. "You need help. Let me get you help."

Would he have been sober enough to hear me? Even if he were, would my words have mattered? Warren told him those very words a hundred times, and in the end, it was Warren who ended up leaving, not Johnny who ended up going to rehab. Difficult though it is to admit, I am unsure that I possessed the skill, the words, the knowledge, or the relationship needed to do for Johnny what he was unable to do for himself.

What is it that causes this disconnect for me between knowing what it means to be a good neighbor and actually being one to someone like Johnny? I want to blame it on New England snobbery and urban living, this fast-paced, closed-door existence that leaves no time for sitting on porches, no space for holding people as they struggle. I want to indict our society's flawed approach towards addiction. I want it not to be a personal failing that has caused me to fail Johnny, and yet I'm not entirely convinced this is the case.

Until COVID-19 hit, Boylston Street felt most like Pamela Circle during a blizzard. Then, Joe from across the street pulled out his snowblower and cleared the sidewalks for everyone on the block, the way Mr. Starcher used to loan out his pickup truck for all of the neighborhood to haul away brush. Then, Anne from next door invited us over for tea, or we asked her over for an impromptu dinner, the way my mom used to walk down to the Carneys' house for a cup of coffee, or Mr. Turner used to come over on Fridays for pizza. Then, I kept shoveling past my patch of concrete to clear

the way for the folks from the clown house, the way I used
to clear the driveways of the elderly on Pamela Circle, even
when they told me that doing so was "bad for my ovaries."
I would think, in those moments, that we knew how to be
good neighbors to each other when faced with natural calamity here on Boylston Street. Human calamity, it seemed, was
more difficult to navigate.

* * *

A few months after Johnny moved out, Warren called me. I
knew what had happened the moment I saw his number on
my missed calls. He told me that he hadn't heard from Johnny
in several days, went to check on him at the new apartment
he'd moved into, and found him unresponsive. That though
there would be no autopsy, the EMTs suggested the cause of
death was liver failure. I wondered if in fact he had suffered
another seizure, choked on his tongue because none of us was
there to call 911.

I sat in my car on the phone with Warren for an hour.
Listened as he talked about Johnny's downward spiral
after moving out. As he recounted that the last two numbers Johnny dialed before dying were his and that of a rehab
facility in Vermont. I learned that he was twenty-five, and
Johnny forty-five, when they first got together. That their
relationship, so ravaged by alcoholism, was the only serious
one he had ever been in. He talked about spending time with
his brother and his brother's girlfriend after Johnny's death
because he didn't want to be alone. About watching them
cook dinner together, and realizing that his relationship with
Johnny had never felt that balanced. Warren's voice was full
of caregiver's guilt, and no matter how hard I tried to absolve
him, that guilt never dissipated. Before he hung up, he told
me he was planning Johnny's memorial service because there
was no one else to plan it.

"Have you ever talked to a counselor about your relationship?" I asked.

"You're the first person I've ever said these things to," he told me. "And given how much better I feel after this conversation, I'm wondering if maybe I should go to see someone."

I never found the right way to support Johnny. Perhaps some situations are too complex for even the most willing neighbor to navigate alone. But for supporting Warren, at least, the lessons I learned on Pamela Circle still held true. Be present. Listen well. Share your bounties. Look for ways to help.

Since Johnny's death, and since the onset of the pandemic, these lessons have only become more pertinent. The early months of lockdown kept us home, and our neighbors became our only regular source of socially distant contact. Together with our neighbors, we built and cared for a massive community garden in Anne's yard—raised beds of kale and squash and tomatoes so copious in their yield that we struggled to find uses for it all. When Laura and I cooked up batches of dumplings or pots of soup too large for us to consume alone, we dropped containers off at the doorsteps of friends who live down the street and around the corner. We picked up Anne's prescriptions and groceries to keep her out of the stores. Laura's colleague Zach brought us the results of his bread-making experiments. Anne gave us mason jars full of smoothies made from kale in her garden. Craig and Sarah invited us to sit in the backyard at their firepit and share wine and cheese at the end of many workweeks.

At one point during an elaborate weekend cooking session which entailed listening to WWOZ and making dumplings to share with our neighbors, Laura remarked, "I get it now. I get what you did growing up. I get what people do when they don't live in the city." And suddenly, it was as though I was back on Pamela Circle, with its bulging bags of produce, its plates of cookies, its porches made just for visiting.

For all the challenges the pandemic has thrown at us, there has been this realization too: that we can slow down when forced to. That we can care for each other when the moment demands it of us. That our failure to neighbor is not a failure of character; it is a failure of the way our society is designed. So it is that I cling to the possibility that the neighboring of Pamela Circle, the love and connection that existed in that space, can exist on Boylston Street too. That the lessons of my past, and of this pandemic, can show us a slower, kinder way forward, with neighbors who see and know and love each other, and can bolster one another when we struggle.

☉☉☉☉☉☉

The Hindu Hillbilly Spice Company: Indolachian Flavors Blend

🌱 🌿 🌱

☉☉☉☉☉☉

··

All about Indolachian Flavors

··

What happens when you drop one hundred Indian families in a river valley deep in the heart of Appalachia? How does their culture and cuisine persist? How do their tastes shift and change in relation to the tastes of the place where they settled? This spice collection contains the flavors of western Gujarat, rural Appalachia, and the place where those collide: on West Virginia kitchen tables where food and love are forever intertwined. The secret mix of spices in our dhana jiru that makes every meal taste like mom's cooking. The ramp salt made from foraged wild ramps found deep in West Virginia forests. The unmistakable color and fragrance of turmeric that leaves your fingers stained bright yellow. Each freshly ground blend transports you to a place—an intersection of cultures and cuisines—that no one else in America seems to know exists at all. Read more about the spices in this unique collection.

Contents

DHANA JIRU

Ingredients
Organic cumin, organic coriander, organic cloves

Food Complements
Your mom's fried okra, the most cultural crossover vegetable (or is it a fruit?) in existence; pan-fried potatoes cooked on rainy mornings; banana peppers fresh from the garden, stuffed with dhana jiru and then seared on a cast iron skillet.

Optimum Freshness
Ground by your mother in her coffee grinder, and sent or brought to you in Ziploc bags not strong enough to trap the aromas, this spice mix will last up to six months in the pantry, while its scent will last for weeks on your clothes and years in your house.

Storage
To maximize freshness, store in one of the many mason jars in your pantry. Transfer only a few tablespoons a time into your masaliyu, the stainless-steel spice tin that marks Indian kitchens, much as mason jars mark Appalachian ones.

RAMP SALT

———

Ingredients
Organic ramps, organic salt mined from the Kanawha Salines just miles from where you grew up

Food Complements
Garden tomatoes picked under the early morning southern summer sun, soups your mom learned to make from her West Virginian friends and neighbors, fresh corn harvested in August and shared at the annual "corn party" in the backyard of your childhood home, where Indian aunties and uncles, and Pamela Circle neighbors, would gather to consume an overwhelming harvest. Because when the corn silks turn dark and the corn comes in, it all comes at once.

Optimum Freshness
Ramps can only be harvested for a few short weeks in April, by dogged hunters who refuse to share the secret spots where these alliums can be found. Or they can be purchased at your local Whole Foods for $18/pound. Either way, once dried and ground, this spice mix will last up to six months.

Storage
To prevent overuse, when really any old salt would do on most dishes, keep ramp salt in a small glass container in the darkest corner of your tallest cabinet. Use it only when you desperately miss home, miss the flavors, the aromas, and the warmth.

TURMERIC

Ingredients
Turmeric

Food Complements
Lemon rice, which your mother would send you to school with for lunch and which turmeric turned fluorescent yellow. When packed in the Ziploc biohazard bags covered in skull and crossbones your dad brought home from work (why pay for what you can get for free?), it would send the other children running as far as they could from your seat in the cafeteria. Because in addition to being one of only two Indian kids in an all-White school, now you were bringing hazardous waste to eat for lunch.

Optimum Freshness
As evidenced by the yellow stains on your laundry, which do not disappear even after repeated washings, and the way those thirty-year-old cafeteria conversations still make you sensitive to negative comments about Indian food's smell or appearance, turmeric's potency never fades.

Storage
Turmeric goes in the masaliyu. But it also goes in "golden milk" at Starbucks and has suddenly become trendy after decades of being the source of intense shame. Go figure.

CHAAT MASALA

Ingredients
Organic cumin, organic mint, organic black pepper, kala namak (black salt)

Food Complements
Chaat masala goes on everything. It adds a zippy twist to fresh fruit, depth to plain yogurt, spiciness to anything bland. As Indians living in West Virginia in the eighties, you quickly learned that the concept of vegetarian food was nonexistent. Or rather, that being vegetarian meant picking at all the sides while everyone else ate a full meal and then coming home and eating dinner afterwards. Chaat masala, at least, gave some flavor to the boiled vegetables populating your plates when you ate outside the house.

Optimum Freshness
You never need to worry about freshness with chaat masala. You'll run out of it well before the expiration date.

Storage
Put chaat masala in a small vial—one that can fit in your purse or your pocket. It's the desi-equivalent of Beyonce's "I've got hot sauce in my bag/swag."

PICKLING SPICE

Ingredients
Dill seed, granulated garlic, dried chili flakes

Food Complements
Cucumbers, carrots, green beans, beets, green tomatoes,
ramps. You name it, it can be pickled. You learned to pickle
from Mrs. B, your adopted grandmother, who gave you pickles made from garden vegetables at the end of every summer.
And while your mother found more joy in canning tomatoes,
making sauce and salsa, it is the pickling tradition that has
kept you firmly rooted in your Appalachian heritage. Your
pantry is lined with jars of pickled cucumbers, beans, carrots, and cucamelons that you savor sparingly throughout
the winter. Each August, you buy more mason jars, more dill,
more vinegar, and stock the pantry once again.

Optimum Freshness
Once pickled and pressure canned, vegetables will last on
the shelf for a year. But they taste crunchier and better if
instead of pressure canning, you keep them in the bottom
shelf of your refrigerator. Or better yet, if you can convince
your partner to let you buy a separate fridge entirely for the
purpose of storing pickles. Good luck with that.

Storage
Pickling spice goes in the pickling section of your pantry,
along with mason jars, lids, canning salt, and vinegar. A
daily reminder that no matter how far you go from the West
Virginia hills, its traditions remain within you.

○○○○○○

Shame-Shame

🌱🌿🌱

○○○○○○

My twenty-something-year-old cousin, Priya, aspires to be an Instagram Influencer. I feel old when I hear this. So old that, overnight, my bones seem to acquire a creakiness I never knew they possessed.

I ask a former student, David, whom Laura and I love like he is our own son, to help me understand. "An influencer," he explains in the gentle and clear tones of a millennial translating for his aging, hard-of-hearing grandmother, "is someone who wants to be paid by companies to advertise their products on their Instagram feed."

"This is how millennials make money?" I wonder aloud. *Creak, creak,* my aging bones respond.

My sister, seven years older than me, but infinitely more technologically hip, informs me that Priya is already Insta-famous, with over 215,000 followers. She describes Priya's posts in vivid detail: the ones where she poses with her hand barely covering her breasts in front of a tropical waterfall or a gaggle of brown-skinned, mustachioed men or a pile of juicy Alphonso mangoes; the ones where she talks openly of tripping on psychedelics; the ones where she wanders the streets of Thailand or Indonesia or Bosnia barefoot, using her beauty to beg for food and money from strangers.

"Her mom even created an Instagram account to follow her," my sister tells me. "She likes and comments on most of the posts."

My sister shares these details in an effort to liberate me: If Priya can post in these revealing ways, she posits, then I should be able to write without restraint. If she can publicly compose profanity-laced poetry, recruit people to join her Indian Psychedelic Society, discuss her parents' complex relationship, and describe her hallucinogenic trips on a shamanic snuff called hapeh (creaking bones creak even louder with this one), then surely it is acceptable for me to write my essays about growing up Indian in West Virginia; about navigating intersectional race, class, and gender dynamics; about the relationships that have both nourished and starved me.

* * *

There's an image that comes to my mind often: a little brown-skinned, black-haired child running around the house naked, with sweet, dimpled cheeks and a dimpled butt, screeching with joy. The adult chasing behind the child keeps repeating the phrase "shame-shame" in tones that are simultaneously scolding and loving. I think the meaning of the phrase, pronounced with a thick Indian accent as "shem-shem," has been encoded within me since birth: Hurry up and put some clothes on, the adult seems to be saying. Cover up. Put your body away.

I'm unsure of whether this image is a memory or a dream. Still, early, very early, maybe when I was the age of that screeching child, I learned to see my body as a source of shame. To quietly go to the closet in the basement and get the pads without telling anyone when I first discovered the black-red stains of menstruation in my underwear at age twelve.

To throw the Dear Abby sex ed pamphlet "What Every Teen Should Know," which my parents left in my room when I turned fifteen, under the bed without reading it and without asking them any questions about it. To avoid the mirror at all times except when brushing and flossing my teeth.

Now forty-two years old, I am still unlearning that shame. I struggle to be intimate with my partner, to talk about what I need and want in ways that are specific and clear. I struggle to dress in ways that would accentuate any parts of my body. I loathe photographs of myself where the softness of my rounded belly and the thickness of my thighs are visible. The definition of shame I learned, it would seem, runs counter to the one that Priya possesses, if she possesses one at all.

* * *

To be clear, I have no interest in shaming my cousin. She is beautiful in all the ways Indians value: fair skin, waist-length straight hair, long limbs, and curves for days. The polar opposite of my dark-skinned, short-haired, stubby self. If she can make her self-described "digital nomad" lifestyle work for her, I'm happy for her. It is her parents' response that confuses me. After all, her parents are the same people who lambasted me in emails sent to all members of our family for writing a senior thesis in which one essay detailed their fraught relationship and the questions it raised for me about arranged marriage and gender dynamics in India. A senior thesis that was read by all of 23 people, at most, and not 215,000, but was problematic because it could be discovered if someone with tremendous tenacity Googled my name and happened to click through four pages of search results.

When the red-letter, all-caps emails first came out in 2013, denouncing me and saying I was no longer welcome in India, I called my mother. Through tears, I parsed my feelings of being stunned by the toxicity directed at me and being horrified by the shame I had brought down on my parents. She tried to explain their anger by saying, "They're worried that your thesis could hurt their daughter's marriage prospects."

Now, years too late, I find the words to respond, "But her posting a picture of herself naked in a bathtub, covered only by flower petals strategically placed over her nipples and crotch, doesn't have the same effect?"

* * *

The word for shame in Gujarati is *sharam*, derived from Urdu. It has three meanings in Urdu: (1) *(n.)* The parts which modesty requires to be covered; the private parts. (2) *(v.)* To be ashamed; to feel shame. (3) *(v. t.)* To cover with reproach or ignominy; to dishonor; to disgrace.

I thought I understood the definitions of sharam fully, having strayed from them far too many times:

1. **The parts which modesty requires to be covered:** Visiting India in childhood, my clothing choices brought only mockery from my grandmother. She called me jamadar, or police officer, because the shorts I wore reminded her of the khaki uniform worn by traffic cops in Vadodara. I knew that the way not to bring sharam onto my family was to dress in traditional Indian clothing: long pants, a long tunic, and a scarf that would cover my nonexistent breasts. But I refused to comply, until the first time I was groped by an unseen man on a crowded bus in Ahmedabad. Only then did sharam overtake me. Only then did the jamadar shorts get retired.

2. **To be ashamed; to feel shame:** On a visit to Edinburgh with my parents during the Fringe Festival in the late nineties, I convinced them to attend a performance by

a Cuban dance troupe. The two-line description in the program failed to mention that the troupe would be nude for the entire performance. My parents stiffly sat through the two-hour show, their bodies communicating the depth of their displeasure. They did not speak to me for hours afterwards. To this day, we've never discussed the discomfort brought on by being in the presence of naked bodies.

3. **To dishonor; to disgrace:** Even when it came to my family's harsh reaction to my writing, I understood that I broke the rules. I shared stories that weren't mine to share, and I hadn't asked for permission to do so. In some ways, it didn't matter whether my audience was one of twenty people or two hundred thousand: I put words on paper describing acts of sharam that everyone knew about, but everyone wanted to forget.

It is this third definition of sharam where my family's response to Priya's choices confounds. Is it not considered sharam when the only person you are exposing is yourself? Or is the issue of shame somehow connected to one's proximity to a community: insiders don't feel it, only outsiders do? Perhaps Priya talks about her parents without censure on her Instagram because the story is seen as hers to tell. I, on the other hand, am a perpetual outsider: When I used to visit India, my cousins made fun of my hackneyed Gujarati, painstakingly learned in lessons taught in our basement by my mom when I was a child. It wasn't enough that I spoke their language despite living in a state where only a handful of other people spoke it. Instead, they focused on my awkwardness, my moments of disconnection. What kind of fool outsider needs a towel to wipe themselves dry after using the pit toilet? Why was my immune system so weak as to require

them to boil my drinking water? My mere existence, my failure to seamlessly fit in, seemed a source of shame. Once,
an uncle had the gall to ask me, "Why do you even keep
coming here, Neema? Your grandparents are dead. You have
no strong ties. There is no reason for you to be here."

Perhaps my writing just provided the ultimate justification
for an excommunication that had been years in the making.

In my darkest moments of self-flagellation, I try to remind
myself that I am not the first Avashia to be shunned by the
family. My great-grandfather set the precedent. His trans-
gression: going to London to study law at the Inner Temple in
1917. He chose his career as a barrister over his family, leaving his wife alone to raise five children. Although he returned
to India afterwards, he never truly came home. Our holier-
than-thou Brahmin-adjacent caste expelled him because they
suspected him of drinking alcohol and eating meat in the
sinful West. Our family rejected him for embracing personal
ambition instead of family responsibility, and he died alone,
the first bringer of shame. A cautionary tale for the generations that followed: fealty to family at all costs, even if it
meant suffocating your own passions.

I keep my great-grandfather's passport in a frame in the
hallway of my apartment. A reminder that I am not the first
to bring shame. A reminder that there are, in fact, other ways
to live besides in fear of shame.

So many times in my life, I have been asked the question,
Sharam nathi aavthi? Shame hasn't overtaken you? So many
times I've wanted to answer, but why? Why are we so fixated
on shame?

* * *

My parents and I have an uneasy, unspoken truce when it
comes to my writing: I don't really tell them what I'm working
on, and they don't really ask. My father's one request every

time he hears that I've published something is "Please, just change the names of people." Never mind that we made a home for ourselves in one of the smallest states in America, where two, not six, degrees of separation exist between each resident. He wants to be able to hide behind the ambiguity that name changes allow—maybe the person is exactly who the reader thinks they are, maybe they aren't. Even though I strive to write about the people of my hometown and childhood with compassion, to tell stories that are about how people learn to love each other with, rather than in spite of, our complexities, his focus is solely on anonymity.

My mother tries to be supportive of the idea of my writing, even takes memoir classes at the local university and shares her essays with me, but does not understand my need to publish. She wants it to be enough for me to put the words on paper and share them with her and my sister. She struggles to come to terms with my need to share them with the wider world.

I want my parents to be proud of my words. I want them to like and comment and follow, the way that Priya's mother is her cheerleader on Instagram. I want for them, and me, to be free of the weight of sharam, which seems to drive every interaction we have about my writing. I want these things, and yet I live with the knowledge that this is improbable.

Long ago, when I was an undergraduate and first grappling with the stories I wanted to tell, and the ramifications of putting truth on the page, my professor Jane Bernstein told me, "Write with a clearer heart, Neema."

And I did. I took her at her word, told the stories that I needed to tell in order to make meaning of my queer, Brown, American identity relative to the very conservative, gendered expectations of my Indian family. I wrote a book of essays that my dad proudly printed and bound and passed out to members of our family. None of whom, it would seem, including my father, ever bothered to read it until it showed up in a curious cousin's Google search one day.

* * *

In the Hindu epic the *Ramayana*, the action really heats up when Lord Rama's wife, Sita, is kidnapped by the King of Lanka, Ravana. Much of the epic tells the story of the battle to rescue Sita, which, ultimately, Rama succeeds in doing. Still, even after Sita is safely back in the kingdom of Ayodhya, Rama's subjects struggle to accept her. What might have happened to Sita when she was in Ravana's palace? Was she defiled?

Sita's own recounting of her time in captivity proves irrelevant, even after she undergoes the agni pariksha, sitting in flames to demonstrate her purity. The community rejects her, and she enters exile once again. She gives birth to two sons, raises them in an ashram alone, and returns them to Rama when they are ready to assume their princely responsibilities. She subsequently begs the goddess Bhumi, Mother Earth, to take her out of a world that has treated her so unfairly. Bhumi cracks open her flesh to welcome Sita into her lap, then closes over her, leaving the people of Ayodhya alone with their judgment, and their shame.

I've known this story since I was a small child and first read it in the pages of my Hindu mythology comic books. But where my child-self focused on the valiance and morality of Rama, it is Sita's story, the story of her shaming, that I keep returning to in adulthood.

* * *

What are the sources of shame for my family? What are the sources of shame for me? And what do I do when the Venn diagram of those two has less and less shared space in the middle?

We share the shame of my body, it is true. But I do not share their shame when it comes to my words.

Last year, an essay of mine that tells the story of why I no longer go to India was published online. In it, I talk about why the combination of some extended family members' reactions to my writing, their obsequious opinions of a bigoted, tyrannical prime minister, and their explicit homophobia have left me with zero desire to return to a place that once filled me with such joy. My sister discovered it online before I even realized it had been published. She called me to talk about it. First, to say that it was beautiful and that she loved it, and then, when asked about how freely I should share it, to tell me to proceed with an abundance of caution.

"I don't think this is one Mommy needs to see," she told me. And though she didn't intend for it to have this effect, my cheeks grew hot with sharam. I had gone too far with my words, and now I needed to cover them up.

"Eventually she is going to see them. Wouldn't it be better for me to just show them to her now?" I pushed. I am unlearning.

Still, she held firm. "If she finds them on her own, so be it. I don't think you need to put them in her face."

I posted the link to the essay on Twitter, a space none of my family yet inhabits. I emailed the link to a list of close friends. One responded, "All your writing about family is so genuine and complicated. I wish you could post on Facebook and get it out there more, but I guess that's not going to happen, at least for the moment."

When is the moment when the cloud of sharam lifts, I wonder? Is it when all the people whose esteem matters most are no longer alive to feel it? Or is it when the weight of the story I need to tell grows heavier than the weight of my family's judgment? This feels like an impossible math problem I am constantly trying to solve, and never getting right.

Still, my mind returns to the sweet Brown child I was. To the sweet Brown child my niece is. To the sweet Brown child I hope to mother one day soon. I see that naked child, fresh out of our cast iron bathtub, running on the honey-colored pine floors of our apartment, with me chasing behind her. My great-grandfather looks down at us from the aging pages of his passport, intense and unsmiling. My mind flashes to Priya, posing unabashedly beneath the waterfall, free of the weight of shame. I scoop the child up momentarily, kiss her, tell her that she is my heart, then set her down and let her run, her laughter the only sound echoing through the house.

Our Armor

1.

My mother's morning preparations always took the same form. She emerged from the bathroom after her shower, the air around her perfumed by a heady mix of talcum powder and baby oil. Dressed in a blouse and petticoat, the softness of her belly just spilled over the tightness of the drawstring waist. From my perch on her bed, I watched her get ready for the day ahead, following her movements through her reflection in the mirror.

First, she mercilessly attacked the knots in her waist-length hair with a plastic comb, then used her slender fingers to divide the hair into three equal sections, which she braided without looking, only pulling the braid over her shoulder when her arms could no longer reach far enough down her back. Next, she wrapped a sari around her body, pleating and draping six yards of silk with a tailor's precision. Last, she put on her ornaments: thin gold bangles that jangled solidly on her wrists, small gold hoop earrings, a black and gold pearl mangalsutra around her neck, a black mascara chandlo on her forehead.

Ensemble complete, she stepped out of our home and into the wilds of small-town West Virginia. In such a foreign context, she opted to own her foreignness, rather than hide it, on our walks to school, at her job as an accountant, during her service on the board of the local library, as the troop leader for the Girl Scouts.

The chandlo was the marker of marriage for Indian women of my mother's generation. It has many names—tilak and bindi are the two most common—but in Gujarati, chandlo is the preferred one. Placed between the eyebrows, at the site of the sixth chakra, it is said to represent the "third eye" and the notion of hidden wisdom. Indian women in India marked their heads with vermillion powder or with tiny stickers in a multitude of shapes, colors, and designs to match each of their saris.

For my mother, none of these options were available. There was no Indian grocery store where she could purchase vermillion or sheets of chandlo stickers. So, she did what immigrants in America always do to survive: She modified. Bought mascara from Rite Aid. Perfected the art of drawing a tiny black circle on her forehead with a fuzzy, curvy brush. Never left the house unmarked.

By midday, the chandlo would begin to crust, crumbled bits of mascara landing on her cheeks or chin. My mother carried her mascara in her purse. Even at the height of tax season, with its sixteen-hour workdays, at first sign of crumble, she would take a moment to go to the bathroom, wash off the remains of the mascara, and reapply, determined to keep her third eye intact.

I used to think my mother was an embarrassment. Her silky clothes and glittering jewelry contrasted so sharply with the hairspray-stiffened perms and acid-washed mom jeans of my classmates' mothers. Our Brownness in a White world already marked us as "other." Why did she need to heighten the distinction? In Jersey City around this time, White supremacists, self-proclaimed "Dot Busters," chased Indian women down the street, beat them when they caught them. The way to stay safe, I thought, was to blend in. And my dazzling mother, dazzling in both her style and her personality, never blended into the bland linoleum and polyester environs of 1980s West Virginia.

I shushed my mother when she spoke to me in Gujarati in public, its pitch and tone so different than that of English. "Speak English," I would demand, refusing to acknowledge her if she wouldn't. Children can be so cruel, the saying goes, and I was living proof.

I curse my cruelty now, when I can't find the vocabulary in Gujarati to communicate complex ideas. Or when I wear a sari and my mother's stinging response is that I "look weird" because she can't reconcile my short hair with traditional clothing. I want to believe that my message of assimilation, pushed so strongly on my mother, was born of my need for safety—both my own and my mother's. But this safety came at tremendous cost. My mother's saris now gather dust in her closet, only worn on the most special of occasions.

2.

Pamela Circle was never a flag-waving neighborhood in the eighties and nineties. My neighbors' yards did not boast flagpoles; their porches lacked flag holders. Flapping American flags were flown in schoolyards, not front yards. Flapping Confederate flags were flown in yards in other neighborhoods I learned very early not to trespass through. But on my street, the main morning sounds were those of birds chirping and basketballs pounding on pavement, not red, white, and blue bunting flapping in the breeze.

Until late September in 2001, that is, when my parents took a trip to Portland, Oregon. They sat in their rental car at a stoplight downtown when a group of White men approached, banged on the hood, and rocked the car. The men screamed epithets and curses and the favorite phrase of White supremacists everywhere, hurled at those of us who are not White: "Go back to where you came from."

The light changed. My father slammed the gas pedal, charging forward, unconcerned about whether he ran over anyone's feet in the process.

Later that same fall, on a Greyhound bus in Logan, West Virginia, less than an hour from our home, White passengers tackled an older Indian man and pinned him to the floor. They viewed his frequent trips to the bathroom as "suspicious," instead of being the result of a failing prostate. They only removed their knees from his back when police arrived to take him off the bus.

For twenty-five years, precisely the same amount of time he had spent living in India, my father had worked to make West Virginia feel like home. And then, any glimmer of insider status he had gained in two and a half decades evaporated between the hours of 8 a.m. and 9 a.m. on September 11, 2001.

After their trip, my father promptly went to Casto Hardware and purchased a massive American flag decal emblazoned with the saying "Proud to be an American." He taped it to our glass front door, leaving sticky residue marks of many crooked attempts before he felt satisfied that it was straight. Another flag got taped into the back windshield of his blue Toyota van. A third got placed in a holder on the porch.

Six hundred and forty miles away in Madison, Wisconsin, I compulsively went across the street every afternoon to check on the Punjabi Sikhs who ran the gas station, using them as a proxy for my parents. Four days after 9/11, Balbir

Singh Sodhi, a Punjabi man my father's age, was murdered at his gas station in Arizona by Frank Silva Roque, a White supremacist who shouted "I am a patriot!" and "I stand for America all the way!" when arrested. Sodhi's brown skin and turban were all it took for him to be interpreted as a threat. As a terrorist. As someone whose murder was justified.

I did not believe my father's flags would keep him safe, but I could not ask him to take them down. I struggled with his assertion of patriotism toward a country that had only shown me ambivalence regarding my existence, and simultaneously lived in fear of what might happen to my parents if the Confederate flag wavers of other neighborhoods found their way to our street, so profoundly apolitical and welcoming up to this point.

My parents' professional lives as doctors and accountants may have buffered them from the worst of West Virginia's ugly racism before 9/11. I, on the other hand, felt its effects from the age of six, when a chubby, rat-tailed kindergartner approached me in the schoolyard, slapped me across the face, and hit me with the ugliest of racial slurs, illustrating that in West Virginia there were only two categories that seemed to matter when it came to race: White, and not White. And again when fans of the opposing middle school basketball team screamed "Mr. Miyagi" and "Speedy Gonzalez" and "Where's your papoose?" each time I walked onto the court, showering me with trash and epithets, then pissed on our school bus at the end of the game. And again when a high school classmate, with his heavily gelled mullet and black Metallica T-shirt pulled over his enormous belly, called me "camel jockey" and "sand nigger" every day during shop class, and our teacher pretended not to hear him.

Until 9/11, my parents did not question their belonging in America. America provided them work, wealth, the opportunity to live a kind of life impossible to imagine in India and to bring family members in India into its slowly growing middle class. Meanwhile I, exposed daily to the ugliest manifestations of American ignorance, received continual reminders that I did not belong. If the flag could protect my parents from this venom, and from the thick, incapacitating doubt that such venom shuttles to the brain, I would not ask them to take it down.

3.

I can't remember when I began to openly flaunt my West Virginia roots, to wear T-shirts emblazoned with images of West Virginia and the lyrics to "Country Roads," to proudly share every historical and cultural factoid I had collected during my time living in the state and have continued to collect after leaving.

I can, however, remember the first time a White man in West Virginia told me, "Go back to where you came from." At a gas station in Sissonville in the fall of 1995, in between chugs from his forty-ounce beer bottle.

And the second time, on the side of the road in Nashville, Tennessee, in the summer of 1996, screamed out a car window.

And the third time, at Oglebay Park in Wheeling, in the fall of 1998, where a leering cowboy held up his hand and said, "How," mocking a Lakota greeting. He asked me what tribe I was from, and when I responded that I was "not that kind of Indian," proceeded to spit hate in my face.

And again in the summer of 2019, when the newspaper headlines announced that our White male president scolded a group of Brown and Black congresswomen using that very same phrase.

I hate the way my body responds to acts of racism. Where

others are able to stay calm and unaffected, or angrily fight back, I simply disintegrate. My eyes blur, my temples pound, and I catalogue counterarguments in my mind. But my dry mouth, the fear squeezing my chest cavity, prevents me from saying a word.

I want, in those moments, to assert my Americanness. My West Virginian-ness. To pull out the birth certificate detailing my birth at Thomas Hospital in Charleston, West Virginia, in the heart of the Kanawha valley. That muddy river valley, those green mountains, those smoking chemical stacks—they *are* where I come from. So much so that I am writing this essay in a room in my house entirely dedicated to the state of West Virginia. The walls are decorated with a wedding ring quilt, a painting of the New River Gorge, and a map of West Virginia that dates back to the late 1880s. My light source is a lamp from the Blenko glassblowing factory in Milton, twenty minutes from where I grew up.

I want to show my doubters that I am an expansive encyclopedia of knowledge about West Virginia, most of which I learned in my eighth-grade West Virginia Studies course, or have memorized from the actual *West Virginia Encyclopedia*, my favorite coffee-table book. Do you know your state bird and state animal? Mine are the cardinal and the black bear. Can you name every celebrity to come out of your home state? Chuck Yeager was born in Myra long before he flew his plane so fast that he broke the sound barrier. Jerry West was from Chelyan, our Zeke from Cabin Creek, years before he made the NBA All-Star Team fourteen times. Walter Dean Myers was born in Martinsburg before he became a phenomenal writer for young adults. Henry Louis Gates Jr. and his brilliant brain spent their formative years in Keyser. Randy Moss first played football in the backyards of Rand, and Lou Holtz did the same in Follansbee. And Jennifer Garner wasn't born in West Virginia, but she lived there for most of her childhood before kicking ass on ABC's *Alias*, where her code name on missions was often Mountaineer.

There are Americans whose ancestors have lived in the same state for centuries who don't always know as much about their states as I do. This is a fact. And it is also a fact that knowledge is not the marker of belonging in America that I want it to be. When congresswomen born and raised in the United States are being told to return to the places they came from on the basis of their skin color and their last names, I find myself questioning when, or whether, our country will ever see people who look like me, my parents, or my child as American.

In the absence of a body that knows how to effectively respond to racism, I wrap myself in my "Home" shirt, with the state of West Virginia replacing the "o," in much the same way that my mother wrapped herself in six yards of silken sari or my father wrapped himself in the US flag. As though fabric can protect us. As though fabric will make it impossible for angry men to see through the cloth to the skin below.

A History of Guns

⚘ ⚘ ⚘

10: The number of guns in my neighbor's gun rack on Pamela Circle. On occasion, after our post-school snack of pickle sandwiches and pudding cups, his son and I took them out of the cabinet in his den. We huddled in the wood-paneled basement, stroked the burnished metal on the barrels, ran our fingers over the honeyed grain of the stocks. These guns, antiques made and used a hundred years before my parents set foot on the tarmac at JFK after their first transatlantic flight, held me in their thrall. They were beautiful, majestic, something to collect the same way we hoarded the Indian head pennies and arrowheads we found on our walks in the woods. Something I knew would never be found in my immigrant parents' home. Guns were too *American* for our nerdy, Gandhi-loving Indian family. I might turn them in my hands, wrists slightly bent by their heft, for brief moments on lazy afternoons, but I knew they would never be mine.

9: The number of years I've been teaching the Second Amendment to my students in Boston and trying to explain its continued relevance in this era of extreme gun violence. I try to be the bridge between red and blue. I channel my West Virginia roots and neighbors to conjure the pro–Second Amendment arguments, but my Massachusetts-liberal students are born and raised in an echo chamber, and many have seen the impacts of gun violence firsthand. They have a response every time. "We need the Second Amendment to prevent government tyranny," I say. And kids say, "Have you seen what's happening in Syria? Guns don't stop tanks and bombs." I say, "We need the Second Amendment because people love to hunt," and kids say, "You couldn't eat a deer killed by an AR-15. Every bite would be full of shrapnel." I say, "We need the Second Amendment for personal protection," and kids say, "You don't need an AR-15 to protect yourself from a home invader." And though I grew up with guns, though guns did not frighten me when I was a child, I, too, read the *Boston Globe* every day, watch the homicide count in my city tick higher and higher, and think, "They are right. They are right. They are right."

8: The number of miles between my house and Camp Virgil Tate, a massive span of grass and woods where I learned to fish and identify edible plants like sumac and milkweed and spot poison ivy and shoot a bow and arrow and load, aim, fire, reload. Holes riddled the edges of the paper target, stalks of hay flew off the bale it was pinned to, but my aim never improved to the point where I even hit the outer circles of the target. Unsurprising, coming from a kid who couldn't cut with scissors, jump rope, or draw a straight line to save her life. Unnecessary, too, for a vegetarian with no intentions of hunting. And yet, there is this part of me that feels that I have failed. That the inability to accurately load, aim, fire, reload is further proof that I am an imposter in this place where I was born, but am never quite sure I belong.

7: The number of minutes from my house on Pamela Circle to the spot on Goff Mountain Road where my father dropped off the squirrels and rabbits he lured with peanut butter and trapped in metal cages to prevent them from destroying his garden. "I'm taking them to Goff Mountain College," he told me. "Someday, you'll go there too." Meanwhile, our back-yard neighbor sat on the grass in the evenings shirtless, with a rifle perched between his legs. The squirrels and rabbits that entered his yard got shot, not trapped. Last year, when a squirrel—I named him Simon—invaded my house, waking me each morning with his gnawing of wood, covering my porch with his urine and feces, leaving pieces of pizza crust on the railings, I found myself filled with unexpected murder-ous rage. I knocked him off the railing once with a broom-stick. He fell two stories, hit the ground with a thud, and then blithely scampered away. I explored trapping, but learned that wildlife traps are illegal in Massachusetts. And, inexpli-cably, I began to think of my neighbor and his gun. I—vege-tarian, Hindu, raised as a pacifist, with terrible aim—fantasized about shooting Simon. What would I look like sitting on my back porch in Boston, a gun perched on my lap, waiting for the squirrel to scurry onto the scene? "Please don't," Laura said. "You do that here and someone is going to call the police on you in minutes."

6: The number of chambers in the pistol my down-the-street neighbor, just out of high school, used the night he played Russian roulette and lost, sending a bullet slamming into his own brain. I was in middle school at the time. He once helped us build a deck off the side of my friend's clubhouse, a hodge-podge of plywood and wood scraps brought home from the lumber company his dad owned. Compared to my scrawny self, he was the big kid with the hammer, and I still see him straddling the beam, hammering away at a piece of plywood, a white baseball cap on his head, cradling the tender brain that would implode just a few years later.

5: The number of minutes away I was from Tree of Life Synagogue in Pittsburgh on October 27, 2018, when a gunman entered the sanctuary, murdered eleven people, and injured six more. In town for a fiftieth anniversary celebration of the creative writing department at Carnegie Mellon, I spent those morning hours locked in a basement on campus, my mind completely taken up with questions about who was at the synagogue that day. Which professors, which neighbors from my time living in Squirrel Hill, which expat West Virginians now living in Pittsburgh might be affected. We tried to carry on with the reading. I awkwardly shared the story I'd planned to read all along, one about a nighttime outing with young people where we used graffiti to grieve the loss of their peers to gun violence, wondered at its wild inappropriateness, or its fitting appropriateness, for this painful moment. I called Laura during a break to tell her where I was, to explain the shelter-in-place. She asked me, "Love, are you okay?" I did not know how to answer her, how to explain that my body and brain still have not adjusted to an America where guns outnumber people, where guns are not Indian head pennies or arrowheads but rather weapons of a war we wage on each other.

4: The number of times we practice "containment" each year at my urban middle school in Boston—once per term. We've perfected the routine: Close the blinds. Lock and cover the door. Place a green sign in the window if all students are accounted for, a yellow one for missing students, a red one if anyone is injured. Text the administrators a picture of the class attendance. Huddle in the corner, jammed between the sink and the garbage can, with twenty-eight adolescents desperately trying to keep quiet. Or twenty-four adolescents trying to stay quiet, and four farting, burping, and doing anything they can to get their peers' attention. My students have so many questions about these drills: Would we really stay locked in the room if we heard gunshots? What would we do if the shooter came through a side door? What about the rooms whose doors do not lock? Aren't we teaching potential school shooters in our midst all of our strategies and plans by practicing these drills again and again?

3: The number of shots fired at Angel, the sweetest of students, just fifteen years old. Killed on a street corner in South Boston at 11:30 p.m. four Novembers ago. The fourth beloved young person to die by gunshot that year. The fourth funeral I attended where I outlived the person in the casket by a full two decades. He baked me a fruitcake at Christmas the year I taught him.

2: Shots to the head.

1: Shot to the neck.

0: The number of times I want to see, hear, or touch a gun again.

Present-Life Hair

My mother says the hair we are born with isn't our own; it belongs to the person we were in our past life. So what does it mean that my first head of hair—the soft, bronzy-black ringlets of my toddlerhood—is still her favorite?

Once shorn, as dictated by Hindu ritual, to release the old soul and make room for the new, the hair that grew back on my head was darker, coarse, and frizzy. It tangled easily, and my mother's efforts to untangle it each week, sans conditioner (a product yet undiscovered in our immigrant household), brought me to tears each time.

We were strangers in West Virginia, the state where my parents decided to make a home. Strange because of our immigration status. Strange because of our anomalous brown skin in an astoundingly White state. My parents could not control much about how the world would receive my sister and me—the racism, the xenophobia, the sheer ignorance about our culture and faith—but what they could control, they did: our appearance. Keeping our heads down, being well-groomed, not standing out any more than we already did, they thought, would keep us safe.

My parents required us to dress up in "church clothes" to go to the dentist, the ice-skating rink, or the mall. The first time my sister wore jeans with holes torn at the knees, my father's response was "I didn't move to the United States from India for my children to dress the way poor children do on the streets of Bombay." And when it came to the subject of our hair, the worst comment my mother could make about us was to say that our hair looked lughra jeva, which is to say, wildly unkempt.

The message was clear: A good Indian girl was docile and feminine. My older sister conformed to this standard for much of her time at home. But I, the typical second child in many ways, began to push back early: played basketball starting at age six, watched football alone in the basement on Sundays, refused to wear dresses the minute I was old enough to express an opinion about my clothing. Hair quickly became the only point of control my parents had over my gender expression. My regulated hair represented my regulated self.

I am ashamed to admit this, but my mother combed my hair all the way through sixth grade. I struggle with spatial reasoning and with fine motor skills. Thus, the skill of braiding down my back eluded me. It eludes me still.

Each morning, I sat on the peach carpet in her bedroom while she perched on the edge of the bed behind me. She slathered her hands with oil, worked it through my locks, and then pulled my hair into the tight, waist-length braid that can be seen in most photographs from my childhood. To this day, I cannot cook with coconut oil. The smell it releases when it hits the pan and begins to warm, the white congealed lump slowly transforming into clear liquid, reminds me so viscerally of hair.

Long, thick, black, rope-like hair came to symbolize femininity for me. My mother had that hair. My sister had that hair. My grandmothers, my aunts, my cousins, my West Virginian Indian aunties, all had that hair. Every Bollywood actress in the black-and-white sixties and seventies films we watched in my house growing up also had that hair. Nargis. Madhubala. Shabana Azmi. These gorgeous, curvy women, with dark eyes and heart-shaped faces, all had dark hair parted down the middle and plaited all the way down their backs. Their dance scenes in white, rain-drenched saris were my first introduction to what it meant for an Indian woman to be sexy, to be the object of desire.

They defined beauty. They defined womanhood. And they felt so, so far away from the woman I felt myself becoming.

When middle school started, I was no longer willing to be dependent on my mother, and became desperate to fit in with my peers. I announced my intentions to my parents, then walked from my house to My Shoppe Hair Salon a few blocks down Big Tyler Road the week before school started. I asked them to chop off my braid, taking my waist-length hair up to shoulder-length. And to give me bangs. My parents refused to pay for a perm, or I probably would have ended up with one of those too.

In my seventh-grade school picture, I exude all the awkwardness of adolescence: glasses, braces, a silk shirt, and hair-sprayed bangs puffed a full two inches out from my forehead. There is a palpable desperation evident in the photo; a need to find a place for myself in a world where I didn't really fit. Cross Lanes, West Virginia, in the early 1990s was home to maybe seven Indian families total. In my middle school of six hundred, no more than ten of us were not White. And my mother's definition of beauty—the one I learned as a child—held no meaning in the halls of Andrew Jackson Middle School.

My best friend at the time could not have been more opposite of me: She was Mormon, all arms and legs, with blonde hair that flowed halfway down her back. Even on mornings when we had volleyball practice at 6:15 a.m., she woke early enough to wash and blow dry her hair, put it in curlers, let it set, then shake out and hairspray the living daylights out of it. Her hair, her ice-blue eyes, and her pert, turned-up nose made her the queen bee at our school—the standard that all the other girls aspired to. One that I, brown and bowlegged, with my weird, hair-sprayed bangs, knew that I could never reach. But maybe, I thought, being proximate to the object of every boy's desire would somehow make me more desirable.

I watched her execute her morning beauty routine after sleepovers. I envied it, and also knew it was something that would never fly in my household. Not the hair dryer, not the curling iron, not the makeup, not the ninety minutes of beautifying before leaving the house.

My classmates' ideas about beauty, based on the country music singers and Hollywood stars of the day, revolved around pale skin, light eyes, light hair: features that were a biological impossibility for me. No matter how big I made my hair, how tight my jeans, how shiny my cowboy boots, I was never going to look like Reba McEntire or Faith Hill. And trust me—I still have the cowboy hat in a box somewhere to prove that I once tried.

What was I supposed to look like? If neither the beauty standards of my classmates nor those of my mother and her beloved Bollywood stars felt like the right ones, then what models existed in the world for me?

My hair came to symbolize this effort to figure out who I was supposed to be in the world—what look was right for me in a world where the looks that existed simply didn't seem to fit. If you were to flip through an album of photographs of me between middle school and now, you would see that I have had my hair at every possible length, and cut in every possible style, since that first cut in seventh grade. Pageboys and ponytails, pixie cuts and bobs, and at some low moments, haircuts that ranged from looking like a mushroom to a mop to a mullet. Yet none of these cuts made me feel desirable or desired.

Beyond appearance, deeper questions also tormented me: Who was I supposed to desire? Who was supposed to desire me? Many of my White classmates were of the opinion that I should date the only Indian boy in our class. But he and I grew up together, slept at each other's houses, treated each other's parents as our own. This idea bordered on incestuous.

I, meanwhile, thought I was supposed to desire the clean-cut, football-playing, all-American boys who ended up being Homecoming King. The ones who were kind to me, and not hurling racist epithets, but who ultimately saw me as some kind of asexual being, existing outside their schema when it came to dating and desire.

I didn't date in any serious way until I was thirty. I tried half-heartedly, went on lots of first dates with dorky Indian boys I found on online dating sites, but never found a relationship that fit, in large part, I think, because I was still trying to heed the mixed messages about gender and attraction I absorbed growing up Indian in West Virginia.

Until I realized the reason neither my mother's beauty standard nor that of my West Virginia peers felt like ones I could fit into—because I didn't. I didn't conform to the gender norms of either of those cultures—not in my clothing, not in my mannerisms, not in my way of being, and not, ultimately, in my decision to spend the rest of my life with the woman I love, instead of with a man I was expected to love by both of those societies.

In 2015, I cut my hair off for good. After thirty-five years on earth, I finally settled on a hairstyle that feels right to me, even if it doesn't look like anything my Indian family or my West Virginian peers would ever condone.

I've gone to see my sweet Colombian stylist, Luis, every five weeks for the last six years. Each time I sit down in his chair, he begins by asking, "So, what do you want me to do this time?"

And each time, I answer the same way: "I trust you."

When he puts his hands in my hair, there is none of the discomfort I associate with those childhood braiding sessions in my parents' bedroom. Instead, there is this incredible sensation of freedom that fills me.

Like me, Luis is gay. He has no expectations of what my hair should look like, or what I should look like. His only goal is that I feel good about how I look. And when I'm done with a session and he spins me around in the chair to get a look at my head in the mirror, for the first time since those past-life ringlets, I actually do feel good. I look cute. My hair looks sharp. These are not words I ever used to describe myself growing up in West Virginia.

My hair is short and cut close to my head, a spiky crew cut when it is at its shortest, a pixie cut with a stubborn cowlick shooting up from my scalp at its longest, with salt-and-pepper streaks at the temples that are increasingly more salt than pepper. During the pandemic, I even took this look one step further, and let Luis give me a fauxhawk that he then dyed a deep burgundy.

Occasionally, when I'm walking in Jamaica Plain, I will see a younger Indian woman dressed like me, in a T-shirt and jeans, with short hair and a gender nonconforming swagger, and my heart will skip a beat. Because suddenly, I am not alone in this style. There are more of us. And through our very existence, we make the existence of more of us possible. We become our own Shabana Azmis. Our own Reba McEntires.

There are still pangs sometimes, though—moments when I feel as though my decisions have put me at odds with my culture and my family. When I look at photos of myself from weddings and see the combination of sari and short hair, I, like my mother, feel that it looks weird. My hair does not mirror the flowing locks of Nargis or Madhubala, or my mother or my sister. My hairstyle doesn't fit. And neither, in those moments, do I.

I wish, sometimes, that it had been easier to default into my mother's definition of beauty. To wholly embrace that Indianness, that notion of femininity, which feels most like home to me, even as I don't feel fully at home within it. Indeed, the sweetest memories I have of time spent in India are still those when I sat on the floor, braced by the shins of my Umamami or my Manjufoi, and played with the folds of their saris while they worked oil through my hair. I haven't been back in seven years, and I still find myself missing that connection, that intimacy.

But every time I visit my fourteen-year-old niece, whose long hair rivals that of her mother's, she will inevitably snuggle up beside me and run her hands through my short hair, form it into peaks, and then smooth it down again. Scrunch her fingers through it and massage my scalp. Get rubber bands and clips and style it into ridiculous, tiny ponytails sprouting from all sides of my head. I don't have to ask—she does it in a way that feels both habitual and intentional. As if to say that my hair, though not like hers, or her mother's, or her grandmother's, is still enough. That I, her short-haired masi in this family of long-haired women, the only of her masis married to another masi, am enough.

Only-Generation Appalachian

My first approval from strangers as a writer came from Appalachia. I never considered myself an Appalachian writer before this, even though the majority of my writing describes my experiences growing up in the region. In truth, I've always felt uneasy in my relationship to the word "Appalachian." Does it apply to everyone who grows up in the stretch of land that runs from Alabama to New York? Or do you not count if you are Brown, Indian, the child of immigrants who moved to a place out of necessity, loved it hard for the time they lived there, then moved away out of necessity again thirty years later, when work disappeared?

But when a fellow writer heard an essay I wrote about my hometown and encouraged me to apply for the Women of Appalachia Project, which showcases the writing and fine art of women from the region, I applied. And upon acceptance, I felt this familiar warmth overtake me. This sense of welcoming and home so potent I can tell you every time I've felt it: In the bleachers the day I won my basketball league's "Heart and Hustle" award in fifth grade. On a roof in Jamaica Plain on my friend Amy's thirtieth birthday watching the sunset with friends who had become family. At sunset on the dock in Maine when Laura surprised me with mason jars full of salt and artifacts from our life together.

I read the acceptance as an affirmation: You belong with us. You are telling stories of our home that resonate. They aren't just a construction of your own mind as you live in Boston; they are indeed rooted in this place. And the affirmations kept coming: publication in *Still: The Journal*, which features writing rooted in the Mountain South. Acceptance at the Appalachian Writer's Workshop.

Where the response to my writing in Boston was often questions—*Why did your family move to this rural place? Why were your neighbors so kind to you? What was their motivation?*—Appalachian writers and readers seemed to be saying, "We get it. We get you." And that feeling was too intoxicating to ignore.

So, I bought a plane ticket to Cincinnati, Ohio, rented an enormous black Ford F-150 (the cheapest option, for whatever reason), and blasted Dolly Parton during my drive up the Mountain Parkway towards Hindman, Kentucky, site of the Hindman Settlement School. Hindman was home to James Still, the poet who is seen by many as the father of Appalachian writing, for many years. Prior to being accepted at Hindman, I had no idea who James Still was. A more self-aware person might have taken that as a sign. I did not.

Laura had laughed when I sent her a picture of my truck before leaving the rental car office.

"What are people driving by you going to think?" she asked, certain the sight of me—short, bespectacled, spiky-haired, and Indian—blasting country music from my perch high above the road would send a puzzled passing driver careening into a ditch.

"What have people always thought about me in this place?" I wrote back. I've never fit neatly into the definition of Appalachia. The truck simply added another opportunity for confusion to an already confusing mix.

* * *

My tank-sized pickup truck barely fit in the parking lot at the top of the hill at Hindman, dwarfing the little hatchbacks and sedans that surrounded it. And I, walking into the dining room that first evening, felt a lot like my truck must have felt sitting up on the hill.

There's this thing I've learned to do in Boston—a city that should be integrated but isn't. When I walk into a room that is clearly majority White, I count the people of color. If the theory goes that there is safety in numbers, my mind always seems to want to know, how many of us are there, actually?

I never did this growing up in Cross Lanes, West Virginia. There weren't enough of us to count, so I didn't. But in Boston, the classroom where I teach is full of Black, Latinx, and Asian students. My friend group is racially mixed. I know the neighborhood bars where I can go and be certain that I will never be the only Brown person in the room. Thus the pain of being in mostly White spaces is almost more heightened now, now that I know the beauty of being in spaces that are multiracial.

I counted four of us that first night at Hindman. Me, and three Black women. Maybe there were others, but I didn't see them. My brain flooded with doubt as to whether I belonged, and I fought the urge to run back up the hill to the truck, eat my dinner at the wheel with only Dolly's distinctive twang as company.

* * *

Each day during that week at Hindman, I walked into a dining room full of Appalachian writers, 99 percent of whom were

White, and though they were nothing but kind and accepting, I felt myself hovering on the periphery, not able to fully
claim the space.

There were parts of the experience that I knew intimately
because of my eighteen-year immersion in Appalachia. The
way the mist covers the mountains each morning, then slowly
burns off with the rising sun. The solid comfort of grits and
biscuits and tomato pie, pimiento cheese sandwiches, boiled
peanuts. The complex mixture of resignation, philosophiz-
ing, and wistfulness that characterizes any rocking-chair
conversation about the political future of Appalachia.

Still, this idea kept circulating in my brain: I am from here,
but not of here. I came to Hindman because I thought I was
entering a community of writers like me. Yet when I listened
to people talk at lunch about being "eighth-generation Appalachian," I felt like the sole strip miner in a community
of underground miners. Eighteen years in the mountains of
West Virginia may have taught me empathy, and given me
some proximity, but the accumulation of centuries of coal
dust and institutional neglect doesn't settle under the surface
of my skin the way it does theirs.

And yet, when I learned to play guitar growing up, the
music I played was Appalachian folk. When I learned to
speak English, it was with a southern twang. When I learned
to drive, it was on one-lane mountain roads full of hairpin
turns. The food I ate away from my parents' dinner table,
where Gujarati meals were standard, was all Appalachian
food: ramps and fried potatoes, beans and cornbread, taco in
a bag, macaroni and cheese. The culture of Appalachia was
the only culture I knew growing up, outside my parents' culture. To me, being Appalachian meant being *American*. My
Americanness was tied up in my Appalachianness. The more
I asserted the latter, the more I became the former.

Until I went to college in southwestern Pennsylvania, that

is, and learned that Appalachia is the butt of every yinzer's joke. And constantly heard about toothlessness and incest. And got told by a dormmate freshman year that saying "needs washed," without the oh-so-important "to be," sounded ignorant. Then, suddenly, my Appalachianness got relegated to the same corner as my Indianness; something to be tamped down, an accent and way of being to muffle, rather than announce. Only brought into view when in the company of others like me, or when I sit at my computer and the stories that pour out always seem to be about home.

There is this other complicating factor in my relationship with Appalachia: For as many ways in which West Virginia embraced my Indian family—inviting us to dinner, teaching us to garden, driving us to practice, making us part of their lives—it also rejected me regularly through the words and actions of people who were profoundly racist. Who spit and slapped, threatened and harassed, used ice and cow-bells and urine to let me know I did not belong. I don't just feel like an imposter in a room full of self-identified Appalachian writers because of my own insecurity; I've also been made to feel like an imposter time and time again.

But in some ways, I know I also do this to myself. I put myself on the outside. I was three hours from Charleston at this writer's workshop. I could have gotten in my car and gone to see Mr. B, my adopted Appalachian grandfather, yet I chose not to. Because I didn't know how to face him after his election-related posts. Because I've lost the ability to see him, and he has lost the ability to see me, and we do not have blood, or coal dust, or weddings, funerals, and family reunions to force us to find our way back to each other.

Am I from here, or am I not? It depends on who you talk to, and when you talk to them.

It depends on what has happened to me in the moments before you ask the question.

* * *

In workshop one morning, I listened to a woman speak of her struggles around the 2016 election. Life in Appalachia, for her, had become so much worse after Donald Trump's ascent to power. It's one thing to be the butt of America's jokes; it's another to be the scapegoat for all of America's problems. And by being given the label of "Trump Country"—totally ignoring all the non-Appalachian states whose electoral majority went to Trump—Appalachia got saddled with all of the blame for Trump's perpetual nonsense.

"Not all of us voted for him," she said. "But to outsiders, we all look the same. We are all responsible." She talked of the daily pain she faced in interacting with family members, neighbors, and coworkers who unabashedly support a president she personally despises. Of strained and broken relationships she has to physically confront. Meanwhile, I only grapple with the tension through the medium of a computer screen from 753.7 miles away.

Still, listening to her talk caused me to wonder: Is the definition of Appalachian so narrow that it excludes even these writers, their progressive politics placing them outside the bounds of belonging? If they struggle to feel represented by the term, then perhaps my insider/outsider battle isn't generational; it's philosophical. And it's a battle that others—many others, who have lived in Appalachia for generations—are fighting too.

On the second night at Hindman, the community gathered to watch the documentary *Hillbilly*, in which Ashley York, a filmmaker born and raised in Kentucky, explored the media stereotypes of Appalachian people found in shows and movies like the *Beverly Hillbillies* and *Deliverance*—and juxtaposed them with the many complex identities that populate the region. York argued that these stereotypes racialized hillbillies in a way not entirely different from the stereotyping that Black people and Jewish people have been subjected to. In each case, the goal of the stereotype is to enable dehumanization: slavery, the Holocaust, and in the case of Appalachia, the complete destruction of the natural environment and the profound exploitation of its people.

In the opening scenes, we watched York scroll through her grandmother's Facebook page and bemoan the pro-Trump propaganda posted there. And for a moment, I thought, "Oh, it's not just me. It's all of us."

But the difference is that when York comes home to visit her grandmother in the film, they can have a tough political conversation and still say "I love you" at the end of it. My relationships in this Appalachian space feel so much more tenuous. I don't share blood with the people I love; only the geography of being neighbors, the history of our lifetimes together. We don't go back eight generations; we go back forty years, and I've been away for twenty-two of them. Hindman reminds me that I am a shallow-rooted pine tree in the middle of a stand of white oaks, trees whose underground root system grows faster than the trunk and branches aboveground. I, on the other hand, can be toppled by little more than a strong gust of wind during a midsummer storm.

* * *

There is this tradition of Appalachian writing I know very little about. I wasn't taught it in school, and in truth, I have never sought it out until now. Because it isn't the Appalachian story I know. The one I know is about chemicals, instead of coal. About living in a planned bedroom community, instead of in a mining camp or on a farm. About being the only Brown kid in classrooms full of White students; the only Hindu in church camps full of Christians. That is the

Appalachian story I am writing, but it is not the Appalachian story that has been told up to this point.

In preparing for the workshop at Hindman, it occurred to me that I should be better versed in Appalachian writing. I started with Dorothy Allison and Silas House. Then moved to Robert Gipe and Chuck Kinder. It took a little time for me to stumble on the Black Kentuckian poet Frank X Walker and his community of self-described Affrilachians. Walker sought, in creating this term, to name an experience that has existed but hasn't been made visible in the societal definition of Appalachia—that of Black Appalachian folks, particularly those living in Appalachia's cities. In his poem "Kentucke," dedicated to James Still, he writes:

> we are the amen
> in church hill downs
> the mint
> in the julep
> we put the heat
> in the hotbrown
> and
> gave it color
> indeed
> some of the bluegrass
> is black.

In "Affrilachia," Walker pushes us to see a community of people "generally lost somewhere between the dukes of haz-zard and the beverly hillbillies." Walker's community is not my specific Appalachian community, but his poetry fills my lungs with a new kind of air, makes me walk taller when I wear my West Virginia shirts.

"Affrilachia" offers me a way of thinking about this that leaves space for my identity. It lets me push back against the defining of Appalachia, and by extension, Appalachians, as racially homogeneous. If Black and Brown people live in it, and have lived in it, then surely it is not.

So what am I? Indolachian, maybe? Does it make sense for me to name myself as Indolachian if my Appalachian roots are only one generation deep?

What makes Indians in Appalachia distinct, in some ways, is the temporal nature of their time in this space. I am unconvinced that many Indians will remain in West Virginia in the coming years. My parents' generation is moving into retirement communities closer to their children, the vast majority of whom have settled out of state. There is no chemical industry to draw new immigrants, and the declining population of the state means that there will only ever be a smaller and smaller number of Indian doctors coming to work in the healthcare industry. I can't foresee another draw that would pull new immigrants to the state, or encourage the children of those already there to stay.

My Indolachian peers and I are an anomaly in the demographic history of our state. We don't have the immigration experience of our parents. We are West Virginians, born and raised. Our accents hold more traces of our southern heritage than our Indian one. We cheer for the Mountaineers and the Thundering Herd. We make annual pilgrimages to Blackwater Falls and Hawks Nest. We blast "Country Roads" when we are homesick, wax poetic over the wonder that is Tudor's Biscuit World. But we have been told by our parents, in no uncertain terms, that our success is built on theirs and must exceed theirs. So we leave, and we raise our children elsewhere, and as the West Virginians we love slowly die or move away, the state will be shunted to a place of nostalgia in our minds, not one whose conflicts and complications we understand intimately.

* * *

Thursday night at Hindman, I chose to read the essay "Be Like Wilt" at the evening gathering. In the hours before the reading, I reread my essay again and again, full of doubt about how it would be received. Would people understand my yearning to belong and how it led me to shoot granny-style in a desperate attempt to score a basket? Had I characterized Mr. Bradford accurately, without falling into stereotypes? Did this thousand-word piece hold together enough to even merit standing up and reading it?

And then I read. And people laughed at exactly the right moments. And sighed wistful sighs when wistful sighs were called for. And burst into massive applause when I was done. After the reading, person after person came up to me to tell me about their connections to basketball, or about the person who had been their Carl Bradford, or about how they understood how very blessed I'd been to have a Carl Bradford in my life.

The flush didn't leave my cheeks for hours. Even though I've left this place, I thought, and been gone for twenty years, the stories I'm telling still resonate. Perhaps, then, belonging is not as far away as I sometimes imagine it to be.

* * *

On the last night of readings at Hindman, George Ella Lyon, former poet laureate of Kentucky, sang songs she had written protesting the separation of families at the US–Mexico border, while accompanying herself on a washboard. I was struck, as I watched, by her ability to fuse old-time musical tradition with a thoroughly modern and progressive political awareness. George Ella saw through the false choice I had been presented as a young person by the teachers and mentors in my community: stay and stagnate, or leave and grow. She found a way to stay, and to let the hills of Appalachia shape her identity without stifling her worldview.

I don't know the kind of rootedness people at Hindman express, or that James Still expressed in his poem "Heritage":

> I cannot leave. I cannot go away.
> Being of these hills, being one with the fox
> Stealing into the shadows, one with the new-born foal,
> The lumbering ox drawing green beech logs to mill,
> One with the destined feet of man climbing and
> descending,
> And one with death rising to bloom again, I cannot go.
> Being of these hills I cannot pass beyond.

I do not know what it means to possess a love of place so strong you remain rootbound even when the soil sometimes rejects your very existence. My wandering parents, living in their fifth home, fourth state, and second country, certainly do not. I want it. I hunger for it. Sometimes, I even trick myself into thinking I have it. But a dinnertime conversation with a woman whose family has been buried in the same cemetery for five generations quickly reminds me that I do not. And in the moment of self-pity that follows, I consider the fact that while the hills of West Virginia shaped me into the person I am today, I have passed beyond them, my shallow roots trailing behind me as I go.

And yet, shortly after leaving Hindman I learned that Mr. Morris, the father of my best friend in high school, had been diagnosed with thyroid cancer and was scheduled for an operation. I ordered him books to keep him company through his recovery—the same set of books I'd used to begin my own exploration of contemporary Appalachian writing: *Southernmost*, *Trampoline*, *Snakehunter*.

He sent me a thank you note a few weeks ago about how much he loved the books and closed it with this:

I hope you know how proud Diana and I are of the work that you are doing in Boston. You are making real, positive changes in the lives of your students. Please be sure to let us know when you come home to your WV roots. There's always a room waiting for you here. Love, Dad Morris.

And with those words, I am home again. Even if it is only home for one generation.

○○○○○○

THANKS, Y'ALL

✿ ✿ ✿

○○○○○○

Fifty years ago, my parents upended their world and left their family, their friends, their culture, their entire worldview behind to move to the United States because they thought this country held possibilities for them, and their children, that India could not. This book is a product of that choice. I know that it has not always been easy to be the parents of someone so bullheaded, who asks for neither permission nor forgiveness and never seems to do things the way they should be done. Bipin and Rita Avashia, I hope you know how thankful I am that you made your journey, and in doing so, gave me permission to make mine.

To Swati, my sister, thank you for being both a push when I needed one and a buffer when I needed one, for accepting the fullness of who I am with no reservations, and for being a champion of my writing even during the time when I struggled to put words on the page. And to Amari, my twenty-eight-year-younger twin, you are the audience I imagine these stories to be for when I'm writing. Life is best lived at its intersections. I know you'll find your own.

I wouldn't be who I am, and this essay collection wouldn't be what it is, without the love, support, nurturing, and nourishment

I got from my West Virginia family. My deepest gratitude goes to my Pamela Circle neighbors, to my Cross Lanes and Charleston aunties and uncles, to the Bs, the Schrecks, and the Morrises. Your deep commitment to community, to breaking bread together, and to sharing stories are all made manifest in the way I live my life each day.

The small group of people in the world who share this history of growing up Indolachian in the Chemical Valley have received my stories with so much grace, compassion, and positivity. Every time I get an approving email or text about an essay, it is validation from the people whose opinion I value most: those who lived it with me. The list of rejected titles they generated for this essay collection, which included names such as *Mountaineers Are Always Ghee*, *West (by gods) Virginia*, and *Pepperoni Dhols*, would make an amazing essay in its own right. Dipa, Paras, Rishi, Sheila, and Nisha, thank you for your careful reading and your life-long kinship.

I'm deeply lucky to have a group of Pittsburgh writing mentors who have accompanied me on this journey. Jane McCafferty and Jane Bernstein, my writing professors at Carnegie Mellon, taught me my first important writing lessons: Janey taught me how to write scenes, and Jane told me to write with a clearer heart. Both sparked a love of creative nonfiction in me that continues to this day. Thank you both, twenty years after being my official teachers, for continuing to find ways to teach me about the writing life. Thanks also go to Geeta Kothari, whose instruction and feedback at the Kenyon Review Writers Workshop in 2017 and 2018, and steady encouragement ever since, have helped to make this book a reality. Nobody writes a book alone, and I certainly couldn't have written this one without the guidance and encouragement you all have provided.

In Boston, Grub Street served as a critical writing space

for me in the process of creating this book. I wrote most of these essays in classes with instructors Benjamin Rachlin, Ethan Gilsdorf, Dorian Fox, and E. B. Bartels. Innumerable classmates provided critical feedback. Two, Sarah Sweeney and Alexis Drutchas, went on to become founding members of our three-person No Name Writing Group, which saw many of these essays find their final form. They, along with my friends Kate Fussner and Noel Reyes, provided so much of the structure, support, and encouragement I needed to move from writing to publishing, and from stand-alone essays to a complete collection. Thanks to you all.

I queried many agents who did not feel like they knew how to market this collection of essays. But when Derek Krissoff, director of WVU Press, read it, he had no such doubts. His choice of readers for the first draft of this manuscript, Rahul Mehta and Ed Karshner, couldn't have been more astute. Rahul and Ed, the feedback you provided on both content and structure, and your validation of my words, gave me the confidence to revise this book into its final form. Deepest thanks to you, Derek, and the team at WVU Press for how you have shepherded this book forward.

And lastly, all my love and appreciation to Laura, who reads and rereads every word I write and makes every story better for being part of it.